YOU are a better writer than you REALIZE

STRATEGIES
to help release
your anxiety and
write with ease

Ali Mullin

Kendall Hunt
publishing company

Cover image provided by Shutterstock, Inc.

Kendall Hunt
publishing company

www.kendallhunt.com
Send all inquiries to:
4050 Westmark Drive
Dubuque, IA 52004-1840

Contents

Introduction

Every semester, I ask students to rate how much they like writing on a scale from 1 to 10, with 1 meaning that they hate it and 10 meaning that they love it. I get a lot of 5 answers, with the student claiming that they just don't care. The next most popular answer is 2, probably because they just don't want to say 1. Occasionally students will say 8 because they enjoy writing poetry or song lyrics but hate being assigned topics in an academic setting. One would think that these answers would be disappointing to me, but on the contrary, I expect those answers, and I see them as a challenge.

I expect these kinds of answers because I have seen what elementary, middle, and many high school classrooms are like. In many instances, there is a primary focus on grammar and usage and a secondary focus on content. It's no wonder that students are anxious about writing: before they can even get a good idea down onto paper (or computer or tablet or whatever you may be using to write), their teacher is telling them to have perfect grammar, use complex sentence structure, and flowery language. By putting so much pressure on the way the work is written, the students are unable to express their ideas freely, and so they feel anxious about the writing process. They are simply too hung up on the way the idea sounds on paper.

Why do students actually *care* about how their work sounds though? It could stem from the desire to please the authority figures in our lives and fit into a westernized culture that values success (the American dream). From the time we are toddlers, we are taught to follow directions, and if we do, then our authority figures and society in general rewards us. This is ever present in school. Starting as early as preschool, if children obey the teacher, they are rewarded with words of affirmation and affection—maybe with a smile and a thumbs up, or a more physical reward like candy or a sticker.

As we move through school, the stakes are raised, and the punishment for not obeying becomes more serious than "time out." If our work has a mistake, the teacher takes a (blood) red ink pen, and scribbles corrections. Our work eventually results in a letter grade, written in stone on the report card, which the ultimate authority figures, our parents, see as a representation of our success as a young adult. Our school time experience becomes our identity; it determines if and where we go to college, which determines our career choices, and in American culture, we know that our jobs are our identities.

All of this pressure to please authority can often limit original thought, and all this pressure to write with prefect grammar can often limit original content and creative thinking. The intense desire to succeed in American culture inadvertently results in nervous students and poor writing that is more likely to be grammatically correct than make any logical sense.

While I appreciate a beautifully written essay, I appreciate good ideas more. I (and every employer in this country, I might add) value the ability to think critically and communicate effectively. Granted, if an essay has loads of spelling mistakes, the ideas can't shine, so your middle and high school teachers were onto something: the way a student writes is important. What is *more* important than knowing perfect grammar though is understanding how to write your best work that has excellent content and style. Finding that balance can be a real challenge, but hopefully this book will make that process simple.

Writing Apprehension Test (WAT)

The following test will allow you to see your level of anxiety about writing. Being self-aware about your writing process will help you to address any problems and become a more confident writer.

Directions: Below are twenty-six statements that people sometimes make about themselves. Please indicate whether or not you believe each statement applies to you by marking whether you: Strongly Disagree = 1; Disagree = 2; Neutral = 3; Agree = 4; Strongly Agree = 5

_____1.   I avoid writing. (+)

_____2.   I have no fear of my writing being evaluated. (−)

_____3.   I look forward to writing down my ideas. (−)

_____4.   I am afraid of writing essays when I know they will be evaluated. (+)

_____5.   Taking a composition course is a very frightening experience. (+)

_____6.   Handing in a composition makes me feel good. (−)

_____7.   My mind seems to go blank when I start to work on a composition. (+)

_____8.   Expressing ideas through writing seems to be a waste of time. (+)

_____9.   I would enjoy submitting my writing to magazines for evaluation and publication. (−)

_____10.   I like to write my ideas down. (−)

_____11.   I feel confident in my ability to clearly express my ideas in writing. (−)

_____12.   I like to have my friends read what I have written. (−)

_____13.   I am nervous about writing. (+)

_____14.   People seem to enjoy what I write. (−)

_____15.   I enjoy writing. (−)

_____16.   I never seem to be able to clearly write down my ideas. (+)

_____17.   Writing is a lot of fun. (−)

_____18.   I expect to do poorly in composition classes even before I enter them. (+)

_____19.   I like seeing my thoughts on paper. (−)

_____20.   Discussing my writing with others is an enjoyable experience. (−)

_____21.   I have a terrible time organizing my ideas in a composition course. (+)

_____22.   When I hand in a composition, I know I'm going to do poorly. (+)

_____23.   It is easy for me to write good compositions. (−)

_____24.   I don't think I write as well as most other people. (+)

_____25.   I don't like my compositions to be evaluated. (+)

_____26.   I'm not good at writing. (+)

From Research in the Teaching of English, Winter 1975, Volume 9, Issue 3 by John A. Daly and Michael D. Miller. Copyright © 1975 by National Council of Teachers of English.

How to Calculate and Read Your Score

To determine your score, first, add together all point values for positive statements (+) only. Second, add together all point values for negative statements (–) only. Then place those scores into the following formula to discover your Writing Apprehension (WA) score:

$$WA = 78 + \text{positive statements} - \text{negative statements}$$

Positive statement questions → indicated with (+) = 1; 4; 5; 7; 8; 13; 16; 18; 21; 22; 24; 25; 26

Negative statement questions → indicated with (–) = 2; 3; 6; 9; 10; 11; 12; 14; 15; 17; 19; 20; 23

Writing Apprehension scores may range from 26 to 130. The following general observations may be made about scores in certain ranges, and only general observations, but note that the further a score is from the mean of 78, the more likely the description of a range of scores will apply.

Range 60–96:

Most students who score in this range do not experience a significantly unusual level of writing apprehension. However, the closer the score to the limits of this range—that is, scores close to 60 and 96—the more apt you are to experience feelings or behaviors characteristic of the next range of scores. A score of 78 places you as a writer on the mean, which is the middle point between two extremes, or **conditions** recorded in a large sample of students. The closer you are to the mean, the better. Nonetheless, you should be alert to the fact that you may manifest signs of writing apprehension in performing certain writing tasks or in writing with varying purposes for different types of audiences. While you may not experience harmful apprehension while writing an expository essay, for example, you may experience excessive apprehension writing a placement essay for faceless evaluators or in writing an in-class essay exam for a history professor.

Range 97–130:

A score in this range indicates that you have a low level of writing apprehension. The higher your score in this range, the more troublesome your lack of apprehension. You may not be motivated to listen or read carefully your assignments, to pay attention to due dates, to remember criteria for evaluation, or to act upon recommendations that might improve subsequent drafts of your essays. You do not fear writing or evaluation of writing, but you may not be adequately motivated to work on your writing.

Range 26–59:

A score in this range indicates you have a high level of writing apprehension. The lower your score in this range, the more severe your anxiety. You are nervous about writing and fearful of evaluation. In fact, research shows that those who score extremely low in this range will not take a course, select a major, or accept a job they know involves writing.

How to Understand Your Score

If your score indicates either low or high levels of writing apprehension, then look closely on the questionnaire to see if you can determine which component(s) of the writing process you need to more closely monitor. Most problems of this kind fall into three main categories:

* evaluation apprehension
* stress apprehension
* product apprehension

When these specific components of writing apprehension are cross-referenced with your scoring level information, you will receive further insight into your particular attitudes toward writing and toward the evaluation of your writing.

Student writers who experience evaluation apprehension expect to do poorly in composition courses even before the courses begin. You feel as though the teacher will give you a poor grade because you cannot express your ideas clearly. As a result, you often claim to be nervous about writing, dislike showing or talking about your writing even to friends, and do not like seeing your ideas expressed in writing. If you are evaluation apprehensive you believe other students more clearly and, as a result, receive higher grades than you do.

Questions that you should examine to help you determine if you are evaluation apprehensive are 2, 5, 9, 11, 12, 13, 14, 16, 18, 19, 20, 22, 23, 24, and 25.

Those student writers who encounter stress apprehension experience fear early in the writing process, sometimes even before they have written anything. You often procrastinate and report that you do not look forward to beginning a piece of writing, even one required for a course. You experience writer's block. Your hands may cramp soon after you begin a timed writing exercise. Once you are able to begin writing, you claim to run into great difficulty organizing your thoughts.

Questions that you should examine to help you determine if you are stress apprehensive are 1, 3, 7, 10, 15, 21, and 26.

For those students who experience product apprehension, the problem does not exist at a particular stage in the writing process (as with evaluation apprehension) or with a particular skill such as invention (as in stress apprehension). Rather, product apprehensives claim that expressing ideas through writing is a waste of time. Such student writers do not clearly envision an audience or a purpose for academic writing. If you are one of these writers, you tend to compose a single draft only, yet you feel uneasy about submitting an essay for a grade.

Questions corresponding to product apprehension are 6, 8, and 17.

Diagnosing your writing process problems will not automatically alleviate them, of course. But the information gleaned from the Daly-Miller questionnaire allows you to anticipate your particular needs and to devise strategies for reducing stress that often inhibits the development of cognitive skills.

Question for Discussion

- Reflect on your WAT Score. Did it surprise you in any way? Why or why not?

CHAPTER 1

You Are a Better *Writer* than you Realize

The first part of this chapter includes several narratives on writing and the writing process, along with some questions to get you thinking about your own process.

The second part covers what scholars call "The Rhetorical Situation." Taking a step back from your own situation, which might sound something like: "I need to finish this essay by 7 am!!" and examining the *rhetorical situation* can actually make writing much easier.

The final portion discusses critical thinking and reading. Once those skills are mastered, writing academic essays will become much easier. Hopefully this chapter and book overall will allow you to see that you are a better writer than you realize.

Questions for Discussion

1. How have your past writing or literary experiences shaped your student-identity today?
2. What is your first memory of writing? Who was involved? Where were you? How old were you? How did you feel about it?
3. How do you think this experience impacted your career as a student?

Narratives on Writing

Reading and Examining Calkins' *Lessons from a Child*

In the introduction, we learned a bit about the origin of the tendency to focus on style instead of content, and we can see a concrete example of this in Susie, a fourth grader, described in Lucy McCormock Calkins' book *Lessons from a Child.* In this example, Calkins observed Susie as she and her classmates did some in-class writing. As the students wrote quietly at their desks, the teacher paced around the room, stopping to assist students when needed. She soon stopped at Susie's desk and showed her that drafts could be messy; "make scratch outs instead of erasing," she suggested.

Like any diligent student, Susie obeyed, but Calkins noticed something once the teacher left Susie's desk: "I watched Susie solemnly fold the messy page and bring out a clean one. With careful letters, she began the story again...Throughout her schooling she'd pleased teachers by being tidy, by doing things right the first time," (45) so this concept of being "messy" seemed backward to Susie.

Eventually, and with some hard work by the teacher, Susie learned how to revise easily, and Calkins observed that Susie "was writing as if there was a tomorrow" (45). She happily drew arrows to indicate a new sentence and made plenty of scratch outs. Calkins noticed that Susie now understood that this draft wasn't a final copy. The scratch outs or messy handwriting wasn't an indication of bad writing; it was just a draft.

Questions for Discussion

1. Even though Susie is quite a novice compared to your writing skills, have you ever experienced a similar feeling when it comes to drafting? If so, how did you overcome it?
2. What did Calkins mean when she wrote that Susie was "writing as if there was a tomorrow"? Do you write "as if there was a tomorrow"? Why or why not?

Examining and Reading Lamott's "Shitty First Drafts"

Anne Lamott, an author and writing teacher, might describe Susie's new strategy as writing a "shitty first draft."

According to her, writing a "shitty first draft" is the first strategy in learning to write with ease. This concept comes from Lamott's book, *Bird by Bird: Some Instructions on Writing and Life*. Read her chapter, appropriately entitled "Shitty First Drafts," to see what I mean:

Shitty First Drafts

Now, practically even better news than that of short assignments is the idea of shitty first drafts. All good writers write them. This is how they end up with good second drafts and terrific third drafts. People tend to look at successful writers, writers who are getting their books published and maybe even doing well financially, and think that they sit down at their desks every morning feeling like a million dollars, feeling great about who they are and how much talent they have and what a great story they have to tell; that they take in a few deep breaths, push back their sleeves, roll their necks a few times to get all the cricks out, and dive in, typing fully formed passages as fast as a court reporter. But this is just the fantasy of the uninitiated. I know some very great writers, writers you love who write beautifully and have made a great deal of money, and not *one* of them sits down routinely feeling wildly enthusiastic and confident. Not one of them writes elegant first drafts. All right, one of them does, but we do not like her very much. We do not think that she has a rich inner life or that God likes her or can even stand her. (Although when I mentioned this to my priest friend Tom, he said you can safely assume you've created God in your own image when it turns out that God hates all the same people you do.)

Very few writers really know what they are doing until they've done it. Nor do they go about their business feeling dewy and thrilled. They do not type a few stiff warm-up sentences and then find themselves bounding along like huskies across the snow. One writer I know tells me that he sits down every morning and says to himself nicely, "It's not like you don't have a choice, because you do—you can either type or kill yourself." We all often feel like we are pulling teeth, even those writers whose prose ends up being the most natural and fluid. The right words and sentences just do not come pouring out like ticker tape most of the time. Now, Muriel Spark is said to have felt that she was taking dictation from God every morning—sitting there, one supposes, plugged into a Dictaphone, typing away, humming. But this is a very hostile and aggressive position. One might hope for bad things to rain down on a person like this.

For me, and most of the other writers I know, writing is not rapturous. In fact, the only way I can get anything written at all is to write really, really shitty first drafts.

The first draft is the child's draft, where you let it all pour out and then let it romp all over the place, knowing that no one is going to see it and that you can shape it later. You just let this childlike part of you channel whatever voices and visions come through and onto the page. If one of the characters wants to say, "Well so what, Mr. Poopy Pants?," you let her. No one is going to see it. If the kid wants to get into really sentimental, weepy, emotional territory you let him. Just get it all down on paper, because there may be something great in those six crazy pages that you would never have gotten to by more rational, grown-up means. There may be something in the very last line of the very last paragraph on page six that you just love that is so beautiful or wild that you now know what you're supposed to be writing about, more or less, or in what direction you might go—but there was no way to get to this without first getting through the first five and a half pages.

I used to write food reviews for *California* magazine before it folded (My writing food reviews had nothing to do with the magazine folding, although every single review did cause a couple of canceled subscriptions. Some readers took umbrage at my comparing mounds of vegetable puree with various ex-presidents' brains.) These reviews always took two days to write. First I'd go to a restaurant several times with a few opinionated, articulate friends in tow. I'd sit there writing down everything anyone said that was at all interesting or funny. Then on the following Monday I'd sit down at my desk with my notes, and try to write the review. Even after I'd been doing this for years, panic would set in. I'd try to write a lead, but instead I'd write a couple of dreadful sentences, xx them out, try again, xx everything out, and then feel despair and worry settle on my chest like an x-ray apron. It's over, I'd think, calmly. I'm not going to be able to get the magic to work this time. I'm ruined. I'm through. I'm toast. Maybe, I'd think, I can get my old job back as a clerk-typist. But probably not. I'd get up and study my teeth in the mirror for a while. Then I'd stop, remember to breathe, make a few phone calls, hit the kitchen and chow down. Eventually I'd go back and sit down at my desk, and sigh for the next ten minutes. Finally I would pick up my one-inch picture frame, stare into it as if for the answer, and every time the answer would come: all I had to do was to write a really shitty first draft of, say, the opening paragraph. And no one was going to see it.

So I'd start writing without reining myself in. It was almost just typing, just making my fingers move. And the writing would be *terrible*. I'd write a lead paragraph that was a whole page, even though the entire review could only be three pages long, and then I'd start writing up descriptions of the food, one dish at a time, bird by bird, and the critics would be sitting on my shoulders, commenting like cartoon characters. They'd be pretending to snore, or rolling their eyes at my overwrought descriptions, no matter how hard I tried to tone those descriptions down, no matter how conscious I was of what a friend said to me gently in my early days of restaurant reviewing. "Annie," she said, "it is just a piece of *chicken*. It is just a bit of *cake*."

But because by then I had been writing for so long, I would eventually let myself trust the process—sort of, more or less. I'd write a first draft that was maybe twice as long as it should be, with a self-indulgent and boring beginning, stupefying descriptions of the meal, lots of quotes from my black-humored friends that made them sound more like the Manson girls than food lovers, and no ending to speak of. The whole thing would be so long and incoherent and hideous that for the rest of the day I'd obsess about getting creamed by a car before I could write a decent second draft. I'd worry that people would read what I'd written and believe that the accident had really been a suicide, that I had panicked because my talent was waning and my mind was shot.

The next day, though, I'd sit down, go through it all with a colored pen, take out everything I possibly could, find a new lead somewhere on the second page, figure out a kicky place to end it, and then write a second draft. It always turned out fine, sometimes even funny and weird and helpful. I'd go over it one more time and mail it in.

Then, a month later, when it was time for another review, the whole process would start again, complete with the fears that people would find my first draft before I could rewrite it.

Almost all good writing begins with terrible first efforts. You need to start somewhere. Start by getting something—anything—down on paper. A friend of mine says that the first draft is the down draft—you just get it down. The second draft is the up draft—you fix it up. You try to say what you have to say more accurately. And the third draft is the dental draft, where you check every tooth to see if it's loose or cramped or decayed, or even, God help us, healthy.

What I've learned to do when I sit down to work on a shitty first draft is to quiet the voices in my head. First there's the vinegar-lipped Reader Lady, who says primly, "Well, *that's* not very interesting, is it?" And there's the emaciated German male who writes these Orwellian memos detailing your thought crimes. And there are your parents, agonizing over your lack of loyalty and discretion; and there's William Burroughs, dozing off or shooting up because he finds you as bold and articulate as a houseplant; and so on. And there are also the dogs: let's not forget the dogs, the dogs in their pen who will surely hurtle and snarl their way out if you ever *stop* writing, because writing is, for some of us, the latch that keeps the door of the pen closed, keeps those crazy ravenous dogs contained.

Quieting these voices is at least half the battle I fight daily. But this is better than it used to be. It used to be 87 percent. Left to its own devices, my mind spends much of its time having conversations with people who aren't there. I walk along defending myself to people, or exchanging repartee with them, or rationalizing my behavior, or seducing them with gossip, or pretending I'm on their TV talk show or whatever. I speed or run an aging yellow light or don't come to a full stop, and one nanosecond later am explaining to imaginary cops exactly why I had to do what I did, or insisting that I did not in fact do it.

I happened to mention this to a hypnotist I saw many years ago, and he looked at me very nicely. At first I thought he was feeling around on the floor for the silent alarm button, but then he gave me the following exercise, which I still use to this day.

Close your eyes and get quiet for a minute, until the chatter starts up. Then isolate one of the voices and imagine the person speaking as a mouse. Pick it up by the tail and drop it into a mason jar. Then isolate another voice, pick it up by the tail, drop it in the jar. And so on. Drop in any high-maintenance parental units, drop in any contractors, lawyers, colleagues, children, anyone who is whining in your head. Then put the lid on, and watch all these mouse people clawing at the glass, jabbering away, trying to make you feel like shit because you won't do what they want—won't give them more money, won't be more successful, won't see them more often. Then imagine that there is a volume-control button on the bottle. Turn it all the way up for a minute, and listen to the stream of angry, neglected, guilt-mongering voices. Then turn it all the way down and watch the frantic mice lunge at the glass, trying to get to you. Leave it down, and get back to your shitty first draft.

A writer friend of mine suggests opening the jar and shooting them all in the head. But I think he's a little angry, and I'm sure nothing like this would ever occur to you.

Questions for Discussion

1. "Shitty First Drafts" refers to a particular writing process. How do you typically go about writing an essay? What works and doesn't work about your process?
2. Give Lamott some feedback on her process. Do you think it will really work in the academic setting? Do you think that it is even useful? Why or why not?

Writing a Shitty First Draft in an Academic Setting

When you write a really shitty first draft, and don't worry yourself with style or format on grammar, when you just regurgitate up the ideas and splatter them onto the page, you can end up with a quite beautiful final draft.

How is this possible?

When you write a shitty first draft, your ideas are suddenly at the forefront, not the stylistic details. In this place of inspiration, when you are thinking so quickly that your fingers can barely keep up on the keyboard, your ideas all of the sudden become clear and concrete. You can see them, and you can feel them. When you focus on content and not style in the first stages of drafting, you will be a more successful writer. After all, it's just a first draft, right? You can go back and fix those comma splices and capitalization mistakes later on, and eventually you will end up with a great final draft. And just a reminder… the teacher grades your final draft, not your first, so why do you care anyway?

Lamott uses this method when writing articles as a food critic, but it also works in academic writing. When college students get bogged down in stylistic details, it can interfere with their ability to think critically. While teaching at a community college a few years ago, I witnessed this tendency often with my ESL (English as a second language) students.

In this particular class, I often asked my students to "free write" to get inspiration for an essay topic. I asked them to just keep the pen moving; write without inhibitions (those nasty voices that Lamott mentions). My most motivated students had the most trouble with this exercise, especially students whose first language wasn't English.

One of my students from the Philippines got off to a great start. She wrote furiously for a few minutes, never losing focus. However, I soon observed her slowly move out of this moment of clarity to a moment of confusion. She stopped abruptly, put her pen down, got out her Pilipino–English dictionary, flipped through the pages for several seconds, and once she apparently found what she was looking for, she put it away. Then she stared at her paper for a couple of minutes, the creative moment completely lost.

Questions for Discussion

1. After reading Lamott's "Shitty First Drafts," what specific advice would you give to this student? Give her a couple of strategies for overcoming the tendency to focus on spelling instead of content.
2. In that same vein, what advice would you give to your future self about the tendency to focus on style instead of content when writing a first draft?

Examining and Reading Carlson's *Ron Carlson Writes a Story*

In his book called *Ron Carlson Writes a Story*, Carlson gives a simple piece of advice to writers when he says:

> The most important thing a writer can do after completing a sentence is to stay in the room. The great temptation is to leave the room to celebrate the completion of the sentence or to go out in the den where the television lies like a dormant monster and rest up for a few days for the next sentence or to go wander the seductive possibilities of the kitchen. But. It's simple. The writer is the person who stays in the room. The writer wants to read what she is in the process of creating with such passion and devotion that she will not leave the room. **The writer understands that to stand up from the desk is to fail, and to leave the room is so radical and thorough a failure as to not be reversible.** Who is not in the room writing? Everybody. Is it difficult to stay in the room, especially when you are not sure of what you're doing, where you're going? Yes. It's impossible. Who can do it? The writer.

Questions for Discussion

1. Describe your writing process. What writing strategies have been successful or unsuccessful in your past experience?
2. Do you struggle with procrastinating like Carlson refers to? If so, then where do you think that tendency originated? Out of fear, laziness, or perfectionism even?

The Rhetorical Situation

The definitions of the term "rhetoric" seem to be in conflict with one another. The term can refer to language that is meant to persuade an audience, maybe in a dishonest way with no intended action to follow. Imagine that during a political campaign speech, the candidate declares, "If elected, I will end poverty in this country!" You may be skeptical because it sounds merely like rhetoric—just words to persuade us, but no real action will probably be taken to end poverty completely.

The other definition refers to rhetoric as the art of persuading an audience in an effective way. Imagine a different candidate who says, "During my tenor in office, I hope to lower the poverty rate by 10% in this city." You may be more likely to believe this candidate; she is a good rhetorician; she is an effective communicator. We will cover the actual reasons for how and why rhetoric can be effective or ineffective in Chapter 4.

Before a writer (or speaker) can create a work successfully, they should understand the situation. This is referred to as **the rhetorical situation**.

The Rhetorical Triangle

An easy way to think of the rhetorical situation is to think of it as a triangle, with each point of the triangle representing a different aspect of the situation. The three points represent the following elements of the rhetorical situation:

1. Text
2. Author
3. Audience

The triangle method works so well because each point is connected—they cannot exist without the others. The text is influenced by the author and the author is influenced by the audience, and every combination thereof. Rhetoric will vary depending on the situation.

Text refers to the message, which may include arguments, data, and information. We may choose to pay attention to conventions, tone, and style for this point in the rhetorical triangle. For example, if you are writing in your journal, the text will be quite different from a letter to your congressmen. You would probably use jargon and more informal language in the diary and adopt a more persuasive tone in the letter to the congressmen.

Author is the person conveying the message. This is the position that you take when you are writing, or it is the position the author takes if you are reading. Understanding the potential biases, background, or interests of the author can help us to better analyze the rhetorical situation. For example, an editorial on an oil spill in the Gulf of Mexico should be perceived differently if the author was an environmental activist instead of a petroleum engineer.

Audience is the person or persons the author is addressing, or it is the position you take when reading. For example, an article written on making the perfect blueberry muffins will take a different direction if it's written in *Living Without Magazine*, whose audience may have food allergies instead of *Bon Appetite Magazine*, whose audience is interested in more upscale cuisine.

Understanding the rhetorical situation in which you are writing (identifying the text, author, and audience properly) will help you to compose and communicate effectively. It will also help you to do a rhetorical analysis, which will be further discussed in Chapter 4.

Considering Context

Let's return to the political campaign speech again. The message (text) in this case is to lower the poverty rate. The speaker (author) is the candidate, and the audience is the voters. How do we decide if the message is worth considering? We need to examine the situation in a bit more detail.

For instance, if the speaker grew up in a poor family, does that change the way the audience hears the message? What about if he or she grew up in a wealthy family? In addition, who exactly is the audience and what are their interests? Does the audience live in government-subsidized housing? Or in an upper middle class neighborhood? Does that make a difference in the way the speaker approaches the topic?

The answers to these questions refer to the **context** of the rhetorical situation. Context has to do with circumstances that create a setting for an idea, event, or in this class, a piece of writing.

Consider the following example:

> A man named David is wearing a baseball cap, a faded tee shirt, worn out jeans with holes in the knees, and running shoes. David is dressed too casually.

Is this statement fair? You can't be sure because you are unaware of the context. We need to understand the setting before making a judgment or argument about David. If David is mowing the lawn, then his clothing is probably fitting for that setting. If David is attending a wedding in a church, then his clothing may not be appropriate.

Before we can create or even understand a piece of rhetoric, it is important to understand the context of the situation.

Consider another example, a list of demands from a husband to his wife:

CONDITIONS

A.   You will make sure:
   1.   that my clothes and laundry are kept in good order;
   2.   that I will receive my three meals regularly *in my room;*
   3.   that my bedroom and study are kept neat, and especially that my desk is left for *my use only.*
B.   You will renounce all personal relations with me insofar as they are not completely necessary for social reasons. Specifically, you will forego:
   1.   my sitting at home with you;
   2.   my going out or travelling with you.
C.   You will obey the following points in your relations with me:
   1.   you will not expect any intimacy from me, not will you reproach me in any way;
   2.   you will stop talking to me if I request it;
   3.   you will leave my bedroom or study immediately without protest if I request it.
D.   You will undertake not to belittle me in front of our children either through words or behavior.

Under any circumstances or context, this list seems to be written by a misogynist, right? Perhaps so. But, if we did know the circumstances, we may be able to understand how it came to be. We may not agree with its content, but knowing the context can help us to understand it.

This list was written in 1914 by Albert Einstein to his wife, Mileva Maric, a scholar in her own right. The sexist list of demands is shocking to us, but by examining the context further, we come to understand how Einstein came to write it.

Albert Einstein was born in 1879. Just five years before he was born, the US Supreme Court denied women the right to vote. During the early 1900s, which would have been in Einstein's twenties, women could not own property, they rarely left the home or were educated. Women were thought of as inferior to men, and were encouraged to be submissive to their husbands. It wasn't until 1920 that the 19th amendment finally gave women the right to vote, which was only six years after Einstein wrote his infamous list.

Knowing the context, which in this case is the history of the women's movement, can allow us to see that Einstein was a product of his environment. He was impacted by American culture of that time period, which labeled women as unequal to men, and this could have lead him to these sexist expectations of his spouse. Granted, we can still have a negative opinion about Einstein's character. It's not as if all men treated their wives this way during this time and Einstein's list is therefore acceptable, but having an understanding of the context has allowed us to see how his expectations originated.

As you can see from this example, one can use the rhetorical situation to understand an idea, event, or piece of writing more fully. Understanding the context in particular can make you a better writer (and reader) than you ever realized.

Introduction to Critical Thinking and Reading

Critical thinking and reading will be covered in detail in a later chapter, but to fully understand the rhetorical situation, a brief introduction to these skills is needed. Understanding the rhetorical situation, including the setting or context of an issue or a piece of writing, is done through **critical thinking skills**. A high level of critical thinking will allow the writer to do *more* than just gather information, put it in their own words, include some transitions between paragraphs, and call it done. Critical thinking and successful academic writing go hand in hand—one cannot write in an engaging and effective way without critical thinking first.

To think critically means to constantly question—to be *critical* of what is being communicated. This is not to say that we should assume that the author is always wrong. Film critics don't just write about what is wrong with a film, they also tell us what was working about it. When we question what we are reading (or being told for that matter), it allows us to develop a more thoughtful opinion.

Practicing **critical reading** can help to develop our critical thinking skills. We read for a variety of purposes. We may read novels for entertainment or the newspaper for information, but with both instances we can also read critically.

For instance, the popular young adult novel *Twilight* can be seen as a romantic love story between an ageless male vampire and a teenage human girl. If we are reading for entertainment, the novel is attractive because of its action, suspense, and romance. If we are reading to be critical, however, the novel might seem quite different—the motherless teen girl desires a much older (100 years, plus) male vampire who must use willpower in order to prevent himself from sucking her blood, which would kill her.

We might read the newspaper to get information about what is happening in the world. A newspaper might have a story on the US president that reads "Mr. Obama was inflexible in his negotiations with Republicans." If we are reading for information, then we may take the sentence at face value. But if we are reading critically, we might notice the author's use of "Mr." Using that prefix instead of the more formal "President Obama" can give readers a subtle clue as to the author's intention, which could have been to undermine Obama's authority.

Critical reading and thinking is an independent process where the reader and student understand that truth-tellers do not exist. Being an effective critical thinker and reader means being skeptical of authority figures, especially those in the media who have the most impact.

Critical reading is the first step in a **rhetorical analysis**, which will be discussed further in Chapter 4.

In short, a rhetorical analysis will demonstrate how the various aspects of the piece work together to achieve the writer's goal, so you may consider the rhetorical situation: text, author, audience, and finally, the context in which it was written. A rhetorical analysis is not a summary, and in fact the reader should already be familiar with the content of the work before they proceed to analyze how the piece is written or being communicated.

Reading Critically: *Colorado Will Show Why Legalizing Marijuana is a Mistake*

Below you will find an article written for *The Washington Times* newspaper and a student's annotations to give you an idea of the thought processes of a good critical thinker and reader.

These notes could be the beginning of a rhetorical analysis. Notice how the student doesn't reveal his or her opinion on legalizing marijuana (that's not the point here), but instead seeks to question and consider even the small details.

Colorado will show why legalizing marijuana is a mistake

American Medical Association opposes pot sales due to public health concerns

> Reading the title of the article would grab the attention of readers because the American Medical Association is an authority on health. If they claim that marijuana sales are wrong, then readers are more likely to believe Sabet's claim. It's a good persuasive technique to include the AMA in the title.

By Kevin A. Sabet
01/17/2014

> The date of this article is worth thinking about. President Barack Obama, a democrat, is in office. His administration is liberal and thus more likely to support legalization, perhaps. This article was written at the tail end of the war in the Middle East, and the economy is slowly recovering at this point. Legalizing marijuana could be a money maker for Colorado, who probably suffered with the rest of the nation during the economic crisis of 2008.

On January 1, Colorado made history as the first jurisdiction in the modern era to license the retail sales of marijuana.

To be sure, there were no bloody fistfights among people waiting in line and, as far as we know, no burglaries or robberies. Legalization advocates cheered.

> This could imply that Sabet somehow *expected* there to be a riot over this new development, but he was wrong. Why would he choose to include this in an article where the purpose is to convince readers that legalization is a mistake? I'm wondering what actually happened on the day that legalization occurred? I should do some additional research on that.

While it is true that most people who use marijuana won't become addicted to heroin or otherwise hurt society as a result, Colorado's experiment with legal pot can be called anything but successful.

What didn't make the news were some troubling developments.

> The author admits that marijuana sales won't hurt society, yet it's implementation wasn't successful. How are they defining success here? Lucrative to the state? Safe to use? Moral to use, even?
> The term "experiment" in this instance seems inaccurate because it implies uncertainty and a chance for something to go wrong. Marijuana is already legal in some parts of the world with a lot success, it seems. Using this term will surely influence readers to believe that officials in Colorado are irresponsible.

By stating "what didn't make the news," Sabet is implying that the media isn't trustworthy. He is claiming that the media is supportive of legalizing marijuana because they didn't cover these "troubling developments." I'm sure that many readers believe that the media is slanted, so this sentence puts the readers on his side. While they can't trust the media, they can trust him. What's ironic about this is that he is the media; "The Washington Times" is in fact a part of the media.

Multimillion-dollar private investing groups have emerged and are poised to become, in their words, "Big Marijuana"; added to a list of dozens of other children, a 2-year-old girl ingested a marijuana cookie and had to receive immediate medical attention; a popular website boldly discussed safe routes for smugglers to bring marijuana into neighboring states; and a marijuana-store owner proudly proclaimed that Colorado would soon be the destination of choice for 18- to 21-year-olds, even though for them marijuana is still supposed to be illegal.

Here he is listing the events that he deems make the legalization in CO unsuccessful. One of his main reasons is that children have ingested it and become ill, but doesn't this happen with teenagers and alcohol frequently? And yet, alcohol is legal. Granted, alcohol presents a lot of problems, but I'm wondering if Sabet thinks that alcohol should also be illegal? With the logic he presents here, it seems that he would.

Another one of his issues is that people intend to obtain it illegally, but again, people do this with alcohol and are penalized if caught. I would imagine the same could be said for purchasing marijuana if underage—one would be penalized.

The claim about an investing group calling themselves "Big Marijuana" seems strange, but again, what makes this a mistake in Sabet's eyes? That the industry will become too big? Some of the largest corporations in the world are tobacco companies. He could do more here with explaining why these "troubling developments" are troubling to begin with.

Popular columnists spanning the ideological spectrum, in *The New York Times*, *The Washington Post*, and *Newsweek/Daily Beast*, soon expressed their disapproval of such policies as contributing to the dumbing down of America.

The fact that other credible authors agree with him makes his point more convincing, but what did these columnists actually write? And what does he mean by "dumbing down of America"? That legalization marijuana can make Americans dumb? Could he be claiming that marijuana is making Americans dumb? Lots of questions from readers may muddle the author's argument.

Colorado's experience, ironically, might eventually teach us that legalization's worst enemy is itself.

This raises the question: Why do we have to experience a tragedy before knowing where to go next?

Sadly, the marijuana conversation is one mired with myths. Many Americans do not think that marijuana can be addictive, despite scientific evidence to the contrary.

What tragedy is he referring to? The child who ingested the cookie? We experience tragedies with lots of products like cigarettes and alcohol yet they are still legal. I'm noticing a trend of failure to explain, and that could hurt his argument.

Many would be surprised to learn that the American Medical Association (AMA) has come out strongly against the legal sales of marijuana, citing public health concerns. In fact, the AMA's opinion is consistent with most major medical associations, including the American Academy of Pediatrics and American Society of Addiction Medicine.

> The AMA must also feel this way about cigarettes, which cause many fatal diseases, yet again, are still legal. I should probably read up on what the AMA says about marijuana exactly, and maybe find out who funds their research to see if there are any biases.

Because today's marijuana is at least five to six times stronger than the marijuana smoked by most of today's parents, we are often shocked to hear that, according to the National Institutes of Health, one in six 16 year olds who try marijuana will become addicted to it; marijuana intoxication doubles the risk of a car crash; heavy marijuana use has been significantly linked to an 8-point reduction in IQ; and that marijuana use is strongly connected to mental illness.

> Finally some concrete facts! These are really scary though, and definitely something to consider. If marijuana really does cause all of these problems, then legalization wouldn't be a good idea. I wonder where he is getting this information though, and the cigarette and alcohol comparison is still valid here: drinking and driving is illegal, as should smoking marijuana and driving, for instance.

> He claims that one out of six teens who try the drug will become addicted, but is that a significant number? I'm willing to bet that 50% or more of teens who try cigarettes become addicted. I keep coming back to the cigarette comparison, so this could be a major part of my future essay.

> Since alcohol and cigarettes are legal and dangerous, marijuana perhaps should not be legal, as it would be more one thing putting people at risk. Is this what the author is getting at? Is the cigarette comparison even valid? I should do more research on that.

Constantly downplaying the risks of marijuana, its advocates have promised reductions in crime, flowing tax revenue and little in the way of negative effects on youth. We shouldn't hold our breath, though.

> Using the term "we" here is inclusive and makes the reader think that the author is on our side.

We can expect criminal organizations to adapt to legal prices, sell to people outside the legal market (e.g., kids) and continue to profit from other, much larger revenue sources, such as human trafficking and other drugs.

> This is a reasonable conclusion. Since the legalization is so new, there probably aren't measures for handling this, and that should be dealt with. Is this a big enough problem to halt legalization though?

We can expect the social costs ensuing from increased marijuana use to greatly outweigh any tax revenue—witness the fact that tobacco and alcohol cost society $10 for every $1 gained in taxes.

Probably worst of all, we can expect our teens to be bombarded with promotional messages from a new marijuana industry seeking lifelong customers.

> He finally addressed what the audience has probably been thinking: what makes legalizing marijuana different from legalizing cigarettes and alcohol? It sounds like he thinks that all three should be outlawed.

In light of the currently skewed discourse on marijuana, these are difficult facts to digest. In one fell swoop, we have been promised great things with legalization. However, we can expect to be let down.

> Many Republicans echo this sentiment during the Obama Administration, saying that the president made promises during his campaign that he never fulfilled. The feeling of being "let down" may be fresh in their minds.

Voters in other states should watch Colorado closely and engage in a deep conversation about where they want this country to go. Buyer, beware.

> Ending the article with a call to action is a nice way to conclude. I notice that he isn't urging the reader to agree with him, but urging the reader to think for themselves and make their own decision. Forming the conclusion that way makes the author seem reasonable and logical.

Kevin A. Sabet is a former senior White House drug-policy adviser, director of Smart Approaches to Marijuana, and author of "Reefer Sanity: Seven Great Myths About Marijuana" (Beaufort Books, 2013).

> I wonder which administration he worked for because that could present a bias. Looking at the content and reviews of his book could tell me more about his motivations as well.

Below you will find another article, this one from *The Huffington Post*, which takes an opposing view point. This time take your own notes in the margins and in the lines below each paragraph. Consider the author's purpose, tone, the perspective audience, and the context in which the article was written.

Reading Critically: "3 Reasons Marijuana Legalization in Colorado is Good for People of Color"

By Neill Franklin and Shaleen Title
01/23/2014

_____

_____

_____

For the first time, President Obama acknowledged this week that the prohibition of marijuana is unfairly enforced against African Americans and Latinos, and for that reason, he says, legalization in Colorado and Washington should go forward. Without explicitly endorsing the laws, he told the *New Yorker,* "it's important for [them] to go forward because it's important for society not to have a situation in which a large portion of people have at one time or another broken the law and only a select few get punished."

_____

_____

_____

As the president acknowledged, marijuana prohibition targets black and brown people (even though marijuana users are equally or more likely to be white). Ending prohibition through passing legalization laws, as Colorado and Washington have, will reduce this racial disparity.

_____

_____

_____

The war on drugs, as we all know, has led to mass criminalization and incarceration for people of color. The legalization of marijuana, which took effect for the first time in the country in Colorado on January 1, is one step toward ending that war. While the new law won't eradicate systemic racism in our criminal justice system completely, it is one of the most effective things we can do to address it. Here are three concrete ways that Colorado's law is good for people of color.

_____

_____

_____

1. The new law means there will be no more arrests for marijuana possession in Colorado.

Under Colorado's new law, residents 21 or older can produce, possess, use, and sell up to an ounce of marijuana at a time. This change will have a real and measurable impact on people of color in Colorado, where the racial disparities in marijuana possession arrests have been reprehensible. In the last ten years, Colorado police <u>arrested</u> blacks for marijuana possession at more than three times the rate they arrested whites, even though whites used marijuana at higher rates. As noted by the NAACP in its endorsement of the legalization law, it's particularly bad in Denver, where almost one-third of the people <u>arrested</u> for private adult possession marijuana are black, though they make up only 11% of the population.

_____

_____

_____

These arrests can have devastating and long-lasting consequences. An arrest record can affect the ability to get a job, housing, student loans and public benefits. As law professor Michelle Alexander <u>describes</u>, people (largely black and brown) who acquire a criminal record simply for being caught with marijuana are relegated to a permanent second-class status. When we make marijuana legal, we stop those arrests from happening.

_____

_____

_____

2. Unlike under decriminalization, the new law means there will be no more arrests for mere marijuana possession in Colorado, *period.*

In the January 6 article "#Breaking Black: Why Colorado's weed laws may backfire for black Americans," Goldie Taylor mistakenly suggests that Colorado's new legalization law may "further tip the scales in favor of a privileged class already largely safe from criminalization." Much of the stubborn "this-changes-nothing" belief about the new law stems from confusion between decriminalization and legalization. There is a profound difference between the hodgepodge of laws known collectively as "decriminalization" passed in several states over the past 30 years, and Colorado's unprecedented legalization law. Decriminalization usually refers to a change in the law which removes criminal but not civil penalties for marijuana possession, allowing police to issue civil fines (similar to speeding tickets), or require drug education or expensive treatment programs in lieu of being arrested.

_____

_____

_____

Because of the ambiguity in some states with decriminalization, cops still arrest users with small amounts of marijuana due to technicalities, such as having illegal paraphernalia, or for having marijuana in "public view" after asking them to empty their pockets. One only need look as far as the infamous <u>stop-and-frisk</u> law in New York, where marijuana is decriminalized, to see how these ambiguities might be abused to the detriment of people of color.

_____

_____

_____

In Colorado, however, the marijuana industry is now legal and above-ground. People therefore have a right to possess and use marijuana products, although as with alcohol, there are restrictions relating to things like age, driving, and public use. Police won't be able to racially profile by claiming they smelled marijuana or saw it in plain view.

3. We will reduce real problems associated with the illicit market.

_____

_____

_____

As marijuana users shift to making purchases at regulated stores, we'll start to see improvement in problems that were blamed on marijuana but are in fact consequences of its prohibition. The violence related to the street-corner drug trade will begin to fall as the illicit market is slowly replaced by well-guarded stores with cameras and security systems. And consumers will now know what they're getting; instead of buying whatever's in a baggie, they have the benefit of choosing from a wide variety of marijuana products at the price level and potency they desire.

_____

_____

_____

Goldie Taylor made the dubious claim that since marijuana prices were initially high in Colorado's new stores, the creation of a legal market won't affect the existing illicit market. But despite sensational headlines, prices for marijuana are just like anything else. They respond to levels of supply and demand. In the first couple weeks, prices were high because only a small fraction of marijuana businesses in Colorado opened, and what looked like every user in the state was in line to make a purchase on the day the historic law took effect. As the novelty-fueled demand levels off and the rest of the stores across the state begin to open, increasing supply, prices will drop. For their money, purchasers can conveniently buy a product they know is tested and unadulterated. And for those who don't want to buy at a store, Colorado residents over 21 are permitted to grow up to six marijuana plants at home.

_____

_____

_____

Make no mistake: communities of color, particularly young black men, continue to face injustice in the form of the drug war, and marijuana legalization has not fixed that. Even around marijuana laws alone, there is much more work to do. But the voters of Colorado deserve to be applauded for demanding an end to the thousands of racially disparate marijuana possession arrests of its citizens each year.

_____

_____

_____

Questions for Discussion

1. What was your critical reading strategy? Did you read the article several times before drawing conclusions, for instance?
2. Did your own personal biases play a part in the way you read the article?
3. Did any part of what you wrote surprise you? How did critical reading *feel* compared to reading for entertainment or information, for instance?

CHAPTER 2

You are a Better *Drafter* than You Realize

A good drafter is someone who understands how important the writing process is. Even though there is a general "formula" (I use that term loosely), the process will be different for every writer. Following your own process in a conscious way will help you to become a successful drafter.

The Writing Process: "Process" Implies Several Steps

Brainstorming

One potential reason why professional writers seem so effortlessly talented is because they choose the subject matter themselves. Students do not always get that advantage; teachers will sometimes assign essay topics, and this is frustrating for many students, especially those who feel conflicted about writing in the first place.

If you are choosing your own topic, then great time should be taken to choose the right one for you. When we enjoy something, we tend to succeed more often at that activity. A strong interest in your topic means that you are more likely to succeed while both researching and writing.

Questions to Consider when Choosing a Topic

1. What are your interests? (This could be something simple like sports, the environment, technology, or the arts. Try choosing something relevant to your chosen major; your research could be useful to your future career.)

2. Is there a current event that involve those interests? (Research it. See Chapter 3 for more on how to be a good researcher because it really is a skill to be mastered.)

3. Write down what you hope to find out about the current event, particularly considering the question "WHY?" in order to develop a context for analysis. (Create a series of specific questions.)

4. The ideal topic will be a controversy, so ask yourself, what is up for debate here? Are people disagreeing on this issue? If the answer is "yes," then the topic will be rich with material to write about. If "no" then perhaps how the issue is being dealt with is more controversial. (For instance, let's say that you are interested in animal cruelty. No one is arguing that we should have the right to be cruel to animals, but people may be arguing about the severity of the punishment for those who participate in cock fights.)

Example Initial Brainstorming

These example student thought processes may help you understand the brainstorming process. You can use this as a model when choosing your own topic:

Darcy's Thought Process

Ok, the teacher wants me to pick a topic. I better make it good because writing on something I hate will be a nightmare. What are my interests? Hmm…my major is sociology, and I'm usually interested in people and their behaviors, not science or anything like that → Have I heard of anything on the news that interests me, the teacher wants to know. Well, I don't watch the news. I did see a five year old and his parents on *The View* recently. He was born a boy, but wanted to wear dresses and play with dolls all the time. His parents let him, but neighbors and classmates were appalled. Can I make that into a topic? → The internet revealed that the boy might identify as a "transgender," but what can I write on with that? Let me search online for the term "transgender" in the news section → I found an article on CNN.com called "Transgender Veterans Speak out on Capitol Hill" that described a protest over the military banning transgender soldiers. Sounds like people are disagreeing with whether or not they should be allowed. → Bingo! That's my topic → Ban on transgenders in the military.

Annotated Version

Sociology major → behavior of people → little boy on TV who identifies as a girl → transgender rights → protesting transgender veterans →

CHOSEN TOPIC: the ban on transgender people in the military

Simon's Thought Process

My major is environmental engineering, so what is controversial about that? I am interested in the environment, but isn't everyone? Recycling is common, and my parents have a hybrid car. Let me search the internet for something like "alternative energy sources"→ I found a site all about solar energy, so I'll search the news for "solar panels" → I found an article called "Couple Invents Solar Panels Meant to Pave Freeways, Parking Lots." That seems like a good idea. Having solar panels on a surface that we already use is interesting, but doesn't seem controversial. → The article makes the idea seem fantastic! This is a no-brainer. Nothing controversial here, really. → Wait. It gives a vague description of installation cost. What if this costs millions? The US is already in debt. This could be a problem. Or, would it save us money in the long term? And where is the money coming from to install it? → I think that I found my topic! → Cost of paving roads with solar panels.

Annotated Version

Environmental engineering major → recycling, hybrid cars → solar energy sources → solar panels → paving roads with solar panels →

CHOSEN TOPIC: cost benefit of paving roads and parking lots with solar panels

The first step in becoming a successful writer, before you ever get a draft down on paper, is choosing a topic. If you aren't interested in learning more about the topic, then your essay will not only be miserable to write, but it probably won't be any good, either. Your disinterest will probably come through in the tone.

As you can see from the above examples, Darcy and Simon began with their broad interests, and after a couple of quick internet searches, they were able to narrow down their broad interest to a more focused controversy. Choosing a controversy that is currently being debated over means that you will be able to find a plethora of sources on it, making the research process more seamless.

Making a Topic Work for You

Sometimes teachers assign topics to their students, and this can be a useful exercise as well. By forcing to students out of their comfort zone, it teaches them how to make something work for them.

For example, let's say that your boss asks you to create a handout for an upcoming meeting. You typically just crunch the numbers, and pass the data off to your colleague who handles multimedia, but she is sick today, so this is new challenge for you. As you sit down to create the handout, you are at a loss. But then you begin to wonder: what would be useful for the intended audience? The people in the audience aren't concerned with specific numbers like you are, but more with overall patterns so that they can make changes accordingly.

Keeping this in mind, you create a pie chart, then write out the conclusion you came to based on the data. The handout ends up being a success at the meeting, and no one was the wiser that the multimedia person was out sick. More importantly, your boss has seen how talented you are, which could lead to a raise or promotion.

Even though you went out of your comfort zone in this case, it taught you a bit about how to address the needs of your audience. Moving forward, when you pass the data along to your colleague, you do in a slightly more organized fashion for her to read through, making her job more efficient and you seeming even better at your job.

By assigning a topic outside of your comfort zone, it can teach you something new about yourself and make you a better critical thinker moving forward.

Let's say that your teacher assigns you this topic: the United States' policy on negotiating with terrorists. At first you are very disappointed. US foreign policy seems too complicated, and you believe that this has nothing to do with you. You are not interested, but how can you make it work for you?

After a quick couple of internet searches, you see why she chose this topic. In 2014, an American prisoner of war was returned to the US in exchange for 5 terrorists to be released from Guantanamo Bay, the US military prison in Cuba. Some people are saying, "leave no solider behind" while others are saying "we shouldn't negotiate with terrorists." You still aren't interested though.

Until….you continue your initial brainstorming with a few more internet searches, and you find a story about hikers who were kidnapped in Iran in 2011. They were hiking to see a waterfall close to the border and were taken. You enjoy hiking, and you too have hiked to see a waterfall before. Not in the Middle East, but you still wonder how this could have happened.

An interest in hiking allowed you to see the topic with fresh perspective. Maybe you will write on how the US and other countries handle kidnapped tourists.

As you can see, topics that may seem dull, too complex, or just appear to not relate to you can actually become interesting. Do some digging, and you can usually find something to focus your energy on.

Planning

Even if it's a general one, having a plan in place before you start writing can be helpful for many students. For some, this planning process can be very similar to brainstorming or even drafting, but consciously considering how you will proceed can be a useful tool. A common planning tool in many high school English classes is the formal outline. Teachers assign it, hoping that the resulting essay will have focus and structure. In theory, this is a great idea. But in practice, outlines can be problematic. Many students will focus more on the format of the outline ("I must have a letter *b* here, so what should I put??") than on the content of their ideas. Being forced to know exactly what your essay will be about before beginning to write can be an anxiety producing moment, and it is one that can potentially stifle discovery of ideas as the writing process continues.

Alternatives to the formal outline are immense: a bulleted list of your ideas, a one page proposal in paragraph format, short descriptions of what your paragraphs might include, etc. However, if you are a person who desires structure, then an outline might be a perfect tool for you. The point is to find what works for YOUR unique writing process and use it.

It is important to note that the plan **will** inevitably change throughout your writing process. If half of the plan doesn't end up in the essay, that doesn't make you a failure as a writer; in fact, quite the opposite. It makes you insightful, flexible, and thoughtful, which are all essential qualities when you're trying to become a better writer.

Even if the plan ends up being useless to you in the end, going through the motions of creating one is a great time to get your creativity and inspiration flowing.

Example Essay Plans

These example student essay plans may help you understand this portion of the writing process. You can use this as a model when creating your own essay plan.

Darcy's Essay Plan

Topic: the ban on transgender people in the US military

Introduction will cover: brief history of LGBTQ Civil Rights Movement, focusing on lawful discrimination.

Paragraph one questions to answer: how long has the LGBTQ community been fighting for civil rights? What rights have they been denied in the past, and what has recently changed?

Paragraph two questions to answer: what issues do transgender people in particular face? How does society view them? Stereotypes...

Paragraph three questions to answer: what is the history of the military's intolerance? Why was the "don't ask, don't tell policy" created?

Paragraph four question to answer: was the transition to allow openly gay men and women to enlist a difficult one?

Paragraph five questions to answer: what are the military's reasons for not allowing transgender people? Are those reasons similar to the ones they had for previously outlawing homosexuals?

Paragraph six question to answer: what are the opponents to this ban saying?

Paragraph seven questions to answer: what are the potential consequences for allowing transgender people to be in the military? Would they face violence, like many women do?

Conclusion will cover: solutions to those potential issues, making comparisons with this current transgender issue to women and homosexuals in the military.

Simon's Essay Plan

Topic: cost benefit of paving roads and parking lots with solar panels

In this essay, I hope to first explain the benefits AND potential negative consequences of using alternative energy sources in general. I will then go over how solar panels work and where they are used most frequently. After the context is well established, I will detail how the idea of paving parking lots and roads with solar panels came about and why it might be a great idea. It might also be useful to write about how the roads in many parts of the country are crumbling, so this could be "killing two birds with one stone," so to speak. After explaining all of the good that this new program will do, I will move into covering the problems, which is cost. I will find the exact amount that solar panels cost and cross reference that number with the average parking lot size to work up a good estimate. Since most roads are built with public money, I will go into the US budget issue, being sure to demonstrate that this could drag us further into debt OR totally bring us out of debt long term. I will conclude with more information on the original inventor of this idea and compare that with what critics might be saying.

Your Plan, Your Format

As you can see, Darcy and Simon have very different plan formats. They chose one that they were comfortable with, and thus were able to focus more on the content of their ideas and less on how to write the perfect plan or outline.

Questions for Discussion

1.   What have been your methods for brainstorming and essay planning in the past? How did they work for you?

2.   What other kinds of brainstorming and planning could be done, other than the ones listed in this chapter?

3.   Explain which student's methods you most identify with. Simon or Darcy?

Drafting

This step will take the longest, yet this is the step that students put off the longest. Knowing that you need to write an entire draft can be intimidating. But who says you have to write the whole darn thing right this second? Why not just start with a paragraph? Start writing on a topic that you find most interesting. No need to start with the introduction, right? It's just a draft that no one but you will read. It doesn't matter where you start, but you just have to write.

In Ron Carlson's words from the last chapter, "The writer is the person who stays in the room." Just stick with it; keep your pen moving, and before you know it, you've got yourself a first draft.

A Case for Drafting "Backwards"

"First thing's first" is a phrase we may often hear. We "start at the beginning" when performing a task. But what if we started from the middle or even the end? How would that change our performance or perception? For instance, if you were to watch the last three scenes of a film before watching the first scene, how would that change your understanding of it?

Take the popular 1996 book turned 1999 film, *Fight Club* (spoilers ahead, folks!), for example. If you were to watch the last couple of scenes, you would see that Brad Pitt's character, Tyler Durden, is merely an alternate personality in the narrator's mind, not a physical being. That understanding would then inform the beginning and rest of the film for the viewer. You would look for subtle hints that Tyler isn't real, whereas someone who viewed the film from the beginning probably wouldn't have noticed. Sure, it "spoiled" the surprise ending, but you were also able to understand choices that the screenwriter made to come to the final, fantastic realization at the film's conclusion, giving you a greater understanding of its meaning.

Let us use this same philosophy when we draft an essay. If the introduction is meant to introduce your central point and the thesis statement is meant to reveal your central point, then should we really write those first? Shouldn't we actually write those last, in fact? Writing is not only a tool for communication, but a tool for discovery, as we discussed in Chapter 1. A student couldn't possibly write a thesis statement first because he or she probably won't know the particular direction of the essay until they finish it.

Beginning the drafting process with the body might make more sense. Once we finish our body paragraphs, we can then discover what our central claim actually is and create our introduction and thesis in a more successful, efficient way.

Just like watching a film starting at the end allows us to better understand it's meaning during the remainder of viewing, writing an essay's body paragraphs first will allow us to see what our meaning, or central claim, actually is.

This way of drafting is more efficient because we will spend less time revising our introduction and thesis as the essay inevitably changes through the writing process.

When students start with the introduction, they often get discouraged while writing the rest of the essay because it isn't taking the direction they thought that it would initially. If we remove that initial predisposition on what the essay "should" be about, then we can remove the discouraged feelings.

Questions for Discussion

1. Reflect on your typical drafting process.
2. Where do you usually begin when drafting an essay? And what is the result?
3. Procrastination often occurs when students attempt to write the introduction paragraph first. Why do you think that is?
4. How will writing the essay's body first change your own essay or writing journey in general?

Creating Readable and Organized Body Paragraphs

Once students have that "down" draft, they will want to be more thoughtful about the essay's content. But when they have finished a couple of drafts and their content is shaping up, it is time to consider essay **organization** and crafting paragraphs that are not only content-rich, but **readable**.

As outlined in the section above, students who struggle with writing academic essays may want to begin the drafting process with their body paragraphs; they may want to *draft backwards*. Most students start at a seemingly natural place, the first paragraph or introduction. Here is why this may be a bad idea for many students: they cannot possibly write the introduction when they don't know what direction the essay will take yet. The introduction paragraph *depends* on the content of the body paragraphs, so you want to write the body first.

Even if students are writing a "shitty first draft" (which they should!), they should keep this general idea in mind while writing their essay's body:

> **I am trying to prove some thesis (or *point*), and the body paragraphs will contain the evidence to prove that thesis.**

The list below will keep you on track as you organize that evidence into a readable, focused essay.

The Four Elements of a Successful Body Paragraph

1. A Focused Topic Sentence

Crafting thesis statements and topic sentences are two separate skills that have the same purpose, which is to provide your essay with an organized structure. The purpose of a **thesis statement** is to allow the reader to predict the outcome of the essay, to explain what the essay is going to prove. The purpose of the **topic sentence** is to predict the outcome of the *body paragraph*, to explain how your thesis is being proven by the information you supply in that paragraph. Each **topic sentence** in your essay should give the reader a good idea of how you are proving your claim or thesis statement.

Topic sentences serve two purposes though: to allow the reader to understand the outcome of the paragraph AND to make a connection to the previous paragraph(s). Focused, accurate topic sentences will give your essay cohesion and focus. It will allow the paragraphs to be unified in achieving a common purpose: proving your thesis.

Take a look at the following body paragraph's topic sentence and content. Reflect on the topic sentence and its effectiveness.

> Even though the latest eating guidelines state that a diet which includes processed meat may be associated with poor health, cancer researchers claim that a specific mention of cancer was left out for political reasons. Susan Higginbotham, a researcher at The American Institute for Cancer Research (AICR) implied that the US government may have been pressured by lobbyists to downplay the risks of eating processed meats when she stated, "As an organization dedicated to cancer prevention, we are dismayed to see that the Dietary Guidelines have allowed lobbying efforts to supersede the scientific evidence, when it comes to meat and cancer risk." (Fox) According to NBC News, Dr. Walter Willett, who heads the nutrition department at the Harvard School of Public Health went so far as to accuse the USDA of censorship. (Fox) It is clear that experts believe that downplaying or leaving out information on cancer risk is not merely accidental, but a blatant omission by government officials for their own political gain. If government officials are omitting health concerns to appease lobbyists, then citizens are left to wonder what else they aren't being told. The controversial red meat health concern may not be due to contradicting or misleading research, but to a lack of government transparency.

> Works Cited

> Fox, Maggie. "Who's Mad About the New Dietary Guidelines? Cancer Experts, For One." *NBC News.* 7 Jan. 2016. Web.

Transitional Language Within the Topic Sentence

Students often use the phrase "the essay doesn't flow" when revising their classmates' work. A "fluid" essay is a readable essay, and a readable essay is an organized essay. Undergraduate composition students typically don't have issues understanding the proper *order* of thought. They typically know how to place ideas so that they make logical sense to the reader. But one of the things that many undergraduates may still struggle with is making connections between their points through transitional language.

In general, most of the paragraphs in an academic essay should begin with a topic sentence that includes a transition which illustrates the relationship between your essay's various points. As you can see from element 1 "A Focused Topic Sentence," listed above, each topic sentence is closely related, but in order to explicitly illustrate that relationship between your points, students should use **transitions** in their topic sentences.

Examples of transitional language are endless, but here are a few: in addition, accordingly similarly, in contrast, although _____ is true _____ also applies, in fact, for this reason, with this in mind, which also proves, because of, instead of, likewise, however, on the other hand, therefore, whereas, conversely, counter to, finally, again, next, lastly, to clarify, simply stated, in other words, for example, in summary, etc.

A good way to think about transitions is to consider them a way to reference what came earlier and introduce what is coming next. Ideally transitional language should be used to show how two or more points are related. Using accurate transitions both between sentences and between paragraphs won't force your reader to work hard to understand your essay's central claim and how you arrived there.

Question for Discussion

1. In the body paragraph listed in element 1 above, "A Focused Topic Sentence," what are some of the transitional words?
2. How are the transitional words functioning to make the paragraph more clear?

Partner Activity

Trade drafts with a partner and highlight every transitional word or phrase that you can find in the first two body paragraphs. Take a closer look at the two topic sentences. Do they utilize transitional language in the way described in the previous section? If they do, write down some notes explaining how. If not, revise their topic sentences to include accurate transitional language. Discuss what you came up with together.

A Balance of Student Ideas and Scholarly Support

Two common mistakes that undergraduate students make in their writing courses: 1) creating essays with too much research and not enough of their own ideas and 2) creating essays with not enough research and only their ideas. The goal is to have a balance of both student-generated ideas and author-generated ideas. Your sources will give you a starting place; it is your job to respond to them, not the opposite. Avoid trying to find sources that are already in line with what you believe to be true, and instead seek to join the scholarly conversation in your essay.

Unbalanced Paragraph

Banning smoking in all public places seems unfair to smokers, yet citizens feel they have the right to clean air. Cigarettes are sold legally around the country, and to essentially ban the use of them is ignoring the rights of a large portion of the country. Alan Hill, a bartender in California told The New York Times, "Smokers have rights too." If a ban like this were to be passed, it would contradict with the laws that are already in existence, which is that smoking is a legal activity. Non-smokers may want a smoke-free environment, which is understandable considering the well-documented risks of second-hand smoke. It only seems logical that smokers should have the right to partake in a fully legal activity without facing punishment, yet citizens should have the right to smoke free air for the sake of their health. This dichotomy illustrates why this issue is so controversial and so far from being resolved.

Source: Terry, Don. "California's Ban to Clear Smoke Inside Most Bars." *The New York Times*. 30 Dec. 1997.

Balanced Paragraph

Laws that ban all smoking in public will no doubt impact bar owners and employees, but the health risks for these employees may be too severe to ignore. Bar owners fear losing business if smoking is banned in all public places, and that fear is certainly justified. In 1997 when California first banned smoking in all indoor public places, bar owners explicitly expressed their worries. One of these worried business owners was Forrest Miller, a bartender at the Studio Lounge in Hollywood who told The New York Times, "I've been a bartender for 35 years, and they're trying to destroy my business." Many smokers (and bar employees, for that matter) feel like bars serve as sanctuaries for smokers who are otherwise shunned from other public places. Of course, the government claims that these bans are simply protecting citizens from the dangers of second hand smoke. However, smoking is still legal, and if people want to subject themselves to the dangers of second-hand smoke for the sake of their bank accounts, should the government stop them? The Center for Disease Control claims that "Nonsmokers who are exposed to secondhand smoke at home or at work increase their risk of developing lung cancer by 20–30%." These staggering statistics are what make government officials feel the need to protect their citizens. Bar owners may be ignoring these risks. When Miller spoke to The New York Times, he brought up an interesting point when he said, "I'm not a smoker, and I'm healthy as a horse." This shows that even some non-smokers do not support this new legislation regardless of the health risks of second-hand smoke, particularly if their livelihood depends on it, as Miller's does. Banning smoking in public will help the health of many citizens while hurting the bank accounts of others.

Source: Terry, Don. "California's Ban to Clear Smoke Inside Most Bars." *The New York Times.* 30 Dec. 1997.
Source: "Health Effects of Secondhand Smoke." *Centers for Disease Control and Prevention.* 05 Mar. 2014.

Questions for Discussion

1. How do the two paragraphs above differ?
2. What in particular is unbalanced about the first paragraph? Too much author or student information?
3. What makes the second paragraph seem more balanced?

Proper Identification of Source Information

Integration of Research: Quote then Give Credit to the Experts

When analyzing and synthesizing a controversial issue, **integrating research** is essential. Learning how to integrate research properly into your body paragraphs makes for a sophisticated essay. Perhaps even more important though is **giving credit to the author.** These skills will be covered in the following section.

When students are assigned a sophisticated and complex topic, they may feel intimidated or maybe pressured to come up with a brand new, totally unique solution to this issue or controversy. While that feeling is admirable, students should remember that their teachers don't expect anything like this.

Let's say that the assigned topic is Louisiana's deteriorating coast line. For undergraduate students, the very best paper will accurately and intelligently discuss and analyze the background on the topic, its various stakeholders, and some of the potential solutions that scientists and environmentalists are working on. Teachers don't expect undergraduate students to come up with the next great theory on how to restore Louisiana's coast line, for instance; that is something that Doctoral students or scholars in the field spend their working lives on.

If *undergraduate* students find flaws in an environmentalists' argument, for instance, or acknowledge strengths in a scientist's solution, then that is certainly a success. Think of undergraduate writing as drawing unique conclusions based on what experts are already saying.

In order for students to draw their own conclusions, they should look to the experts as a starting point. We discussed how to find the best academic sources in an earlier chapter, but we will cover integrating that material seamlessly into your own work here.

Correcting Dropped Quotes

Writing teachers use the term **"dropped quote"** or **"floating quote"** to describe a writing error in which the student drops a quote into a paragraph, making the quoted material appear to be the students' idea or part of their own thought process. This error makes the paragraph much less readable, and correcting student's can be very simple.

Below is an example of a dropped or floating quote:

> The temperature of the Earth has risen dramatically. Most scientists agree that this is a result of human behaviors that pollute the Earth's atmosphere by releasing the poisonous gas, methane. "Methane is emitted by natural sources such as wetlands, as well as human activities such as leakage from natural gas systems and the raising of livestock." (epa.gov) If we do not reduce our methane gas emissions, the survival of the planet could be at risk.

Even though the student gave credit to the source with a parenthetical citation, the paragraph seems dishonest and the quote appears disjointed. While quoting is important, explicitly acknowledging to the reader that you, are quoting a source is more transparent and simply easier to understand. Not to mention, it gives you some ethos for quoting an expert on the topic!

Here is the passage again, but with the quote integrated properly:

> The temperature of the Earth has risen dramatically. Most scientists agree that this is a result of human behaviors that pollute the Earth's atmosphere by releasing the poisonous gas, methane. The Environmental Protection Agency also agrees that human behavior is to blame. In fact, the EPA's website states, "Methane is emitted by natural sources such as wetlands, as well as human activities such as leakage from natural gas systems and the raising of livestock." (epa.gov) Although there are natural causes of methane leakage, we simply cannot deny that our behaviors have an impact. If we do not reduce our methane gas emissions, the survival of the planet could be at risk.

Notice the three steps the author took to correct the dropped quote:

1. She **set the context** for the quote by introducing the author, which is the EPA.
2. She **inserted** the quotation.
3. She **clarified and interpreted** the quotation.
4. She **connected** the content of the quotation back to her original claim.

Activity

The paragraph below includes a dropped quote. Revise it using the four steps listed previously. Remember step four: use the supplied thesis to connect the quote back to the original claim. Information on the quote is also listed below.

Essay Thesis: Although some opponents to Supreme Court's ruling on same-sex marriage believe that state governments should rule on this matter, the benefits for these couples go far beyond the "husband" or "wife" label.

The US Supreme Court's ruling on gay marriage as a constitutional right has supporters of the LGBTQ community rejoicing. As a result of the decision, many couples will now be able to claim their new spouses for insurance purposes. "The logic is simple. Fewer than half of employers that offer health benefits make the insurance available to same-sex partners who aren't married. Virtually all of them offer coverage to spouses [who are legally married]." The jury is still out on whether or not employers are obligated to cover *same-sex spouses* just as they cover *opposite-sex spouses.*

(The quote was taken from National Public Radio's website. Then article title is, "Supreme Court's Decision on Same-Sex Marriage Expected to Boost Health Coverage." It was published on June 29th 2016 and written by Jay Hancock.)

_____

_____

_____

_____

_____

_____

_____

_____

_____

_____

Do's and Don'ts for Writing an Introduction Paragraph

Writing an introduction is simpler than you may realize. The trick to writing introductions (and conclusions) is to *save something for it.* When students are researching their topic, they often put every single thing into their body paragraphs, leaving the introduction overly vague or worse, stating the obvious. Instead, save a few good nuggets of information to include in the introduction.

The purpose of the introduction is to **raise the issue** that you are writing about. In this introductory section, you are attempting to convince your reader that this issue is worth considering and worth reading about.

Logistically speaking, the introduction should actually be a bit longer than you think. One of the most common issues that I see with student-written introductions is that they are just a few sentences long. In actuality, if your essay is say, 6–8 pages long, your introduction should be about 2 paragraphs.

DO	DON'T
…engage the reader with your first sentence.	…begin with a gimmicky "attention grabber" or grandiose statement.
…begin with a highly specific, interesting first sentence.	…start with a sentence that states the obvious.
…clearly define your issue and explain the context.	…give too much away so that you must digress in the body.
…explain why the issue is worth considering.	…draw overly strong conclusions that belong in the conclusion.
…explain and define all stakeholders in the issue.	…include a list-like description of what your essay will accomplish.
…offer a specific thesis statement as the last sentence of the last introduction paragraph.	…forget to include your thesis statement.

Strategies for Writing a Successful Introduction

1. **Quote an Expert or Notable Figure**

    This method works well to lend your ideas some ethos. By quoting an expert or notable figure, your reader will see how important this issue really is. After quoting, be sure to explain the quote. Interpret it's meaning, and explain how the quote is significant in light of your controversy.

2. **Give the Relevant History**

    Start with the origins of the issue and continue until you get to the present. This method allows you to develop a context for your analysis, which we know is vital in the rhetorical situation.

3. **Explain All Sides and Stakeholders**

An issue or controversy rarely has just two sides. Most have multiple perspectives and stakeholders to consider. The introduction is a good place to detail those stakeholders. Explaining all sides of an issue can help the reader to see just how polarizing it is. One strategy for this is to use several brief quotes or anecdotes that reveal the point of view of each stakeholder.

4. **Give a Brief Anecdote**

Starting with a brief narrative or anecdote can both engage the reader and reveal why your issue is worth considering, particularly if the story is true. You could also write a hypothetical anecdote that reveal the consequences of the issue if it is not resolved. Just be sure to follow up with non-narrative information so that your essay is more academic and less like a novel.

5. **Pose a Series of Questions**

Asking questions can allow your reader to see that the answers are complicated and controversial. Once you pose a question, try answering it in several ways, representing all of the perspectives associated with your controversy.

6. **Challenge a Popular Belief**

When readers are challenged by your topic, it gives them a reason to consider it. This strategy will allow you to rebuff commonly held views and give you a starting place to begin your analysis.

7. **Give a Definition**

If you define a significant concept on your issue, it can give your reader clarity. Careful not to start with something obvious though; the definition should be meaningful and highly specific. Instead of merely searching through *Webster's Dictionary*, try using a medical dictionary or other relevant resource to your controversy.

8. **Use Your Second Best Example**

Your very best example should of course be in your body paragraphs. By using a good example in the introduction, it will both support your thesis and inform and engage the reader.

Sample Student Work: Introduction Paragraph

Imagine that you are an elementary school student again eating in the school cafeteria. Your lunch choices for today? Chicken fingers with french fries, hamburgers with mashed potatoes, or fish sticks with tater tots. The school can't afford to prepare healthy meals that include fruits and vegetables. You make your choice and eat your lunch with the only drink choice available: a coke from the soda machine.

The school used to provide skim milk at lunchtime, but budget cuts have forced students to purchase drinks themselves. The next class period, you feel groggy and full, and you even fall asleep while the teacher is talking. At home, your dinner options are much of the same, since your parents often work night shifts and don't have time to cook healthy meals. Over the course of the school year, you slowly put on body fat. At just ten years old, you have high blood pressure and cholesterol for someone your age. You can barely play soccer at recess without getting out of breath, and your grades begin to suffer from a lack of energy to study and pay attention in class.

Unfortunately, this is the reality for many children in the United States. School lunches are often high in calories, fat grams, sodium, and sugar, resulting in unhealthy and non-productive students. Often times, administrators are simply unable to provide the types of food that children need to grow, succeed in school, and be healthy because including whole grains, fruits, and vegetables is simply out of the budget. Parents, particularly those who have low incomes, are also unable to provide their children with healthy food due to the high cost of healthier foods, and they may rely on fattening, yet cheap fast food for meals. So, how do we solve the problem of childhood obesity, and who is to blame for this problem? Parents? School administrators? In this essay, I will examine the childhood obesity crisis and the potential role of school lunches and parental choices in this growing issue.

Questions for Discussion

1. Examine the sample introduction paragraphs above. What strategy or strategies is the student using?
2. Is this an effective way to begin an essay? Why or why not?

Writing Thesis Statements

A thesis statement is one of the most important sentences in an academic essay. This sentence will predict the outcome of your essay and reveal your central claim. Earlier in this chapter, we covered topic sentences. Topic sentences and thesis statements are similar: topic sentences reveal the outcome of a single paragraph; thesis statements reveal the outcome of an essay as a whole.

Writing a successful thesis statement is actually more intuitive than you might realize. Students write thesis statements intuitively in texts or emails. Take a look at the email below. Try to identify the thesis statement in the text:

Dear Professor,

I am very worried about my grade in the course. Unfortunately, I earned a poor score on the last exam and feel as if I may not be able to improve before final grades are due. I would like to request a meeting with you to find out how I can improve my next exam grade.

I think that I mostly need some clarification on the past lecture and perhaps some suggestions on how I can best prepare for the next exam. Any help you can give me would be much appreciated! Could I come by your office at 1:00pm on Thursday? Thank you for your time.

Regards,

Jackie

The thesis statement in this email gives the *reason for writing*. Notice where the thesis is located, what comes before the thesis, and what comes after. This email is much like a mini-essay.

Three Main Functions of the Thesis Statement

Thesis statements should:

1. *Predict the outcome of the essay*

    Academic essays are not concerned with suspense. If you were working on a short story or film script, suspense may be an important part of your work. But in academic essays, readers shouldn't ever feel surprised by the content of the essay because the thesis gives them the final outcome.

2. *Make clear the purpose of the essay*

    Students write for many purposes: to inform, to explore, to argue, to analyze, among others. Your thesis statement should make this purpose clear. You could explicitly state your purpose (I intend to examine…), or it may be implied through your language (this law should be revised immediately because…).

3.   ***Reveal the essay's central claim***

   This may be the most important function of a thesis statement. Even if the essay is not making a specific argument about some topic, your essay always has a central claim. You may want to think about making a claim as drawing a conclusion instead. Your central claim or conclusion drawn could be as simple as "more research should be done" or "this issue is worth considering."

Sample Thesis Statements

Question for Discussion

How do the following thesis statements fulfill the three functions of thesis statements outlined above?

- Public school administrators should modify the existing school curriculum to include year-round classes because it has proven that this method is more successful and efficient than a curriculum which includes a months-long summer vacation.

- A public school curriculum that includes year-round classes may be a good idea for students and parents, but according to recent research, school teachers and administrators might suffer.

- Getting rid of the months-long summer vacation for public school students and teachers has both benefits and consequences that administrators should strongly consider before making changes to the existing curriculum.

- Exploring whether or not year-round classes for public school students is a good idea or not requires examining years of both anecdotal and evidence-based research, both of which illustrate that the answer to this question is not a simple one.

Do's and Don'ts for Writing a Conclusion Paragraph

The purpose of the conclusion is to **synthesize** your thesis. That is, it should restate your thesis, but in its most fully developed form. The conclusion paragraph shouldn't necessarily contain *new* information on your topic but *different* information. It should tie all points together using a final, exemplary example and ideally, it will **look to the future** on this issue. Essentially, the conclusions offers your reader the final answer to the question: **so what?**

One of the most common misconceptions about the conclusion paragraph is that it should contain a summation of the essay's points. This method is very ineffective though. Why *repeat* what you've already written about? While the conclusion should support your thesis, **it shouldn't be repetitive.**

Just like all of the essay's other paragraphs, the conclusion paragraph should make an impact; it should be thoughtful and well developed, not an afterthought. Depending on the length of the essay, the conclusion could be 1–2 detailed paragraphs.

DO	DON'T
…present a culmination of your essay and establish the connection between your essay's points.	….be repetitive or redundant.
…look to the future with your issue.	…raise a completely new point that should really be in the essay's body.
…draw a reasonable conclusion based on the evidence that you already presented.	…attempt to end in a grandiose way. You do not need to give the ultimate solution to the controversy.
…give a final example that illustrates your essay's main point.	…include an example that could undermine your thesis.

Strategies for Writing a Successful Conclusion

1. **Come Full Circle**

   Give your essay unification and closure by mirroring the introduction paragraph. While you do not want to repeat anything from the introduction, you could refer back to a point made in the intro or even expand on an example you gave there. For instance, if your essay begins with an anecdote, try mentioning that anecdote again, but with future-oriented information included.

2. **Explore Consequences**

   Exploring future consequences if the issue is not resolved gives the essay a sense of finality and also helps to support your main point. Consider detailing consequences of potential solutions posed as well.

3. **Pose a Series of Questions**

   Hopefully the essay already answers many of the questions about the controversy. However, some questions will always remain, particularly ones about the future of the controversy, so the conclusion is a nice place to pose those. This gives your reader something to think about moving forward.

4. **Identify Limitations**

   The solutions posed by experts deserve criticism, and the conclusion paragraph is a good place to identify the limits of those "ideal solutions" we read and hear so much about.

5. **Use your Second Best Example**

   This strategy also works for the introduction, but if you don't use it there, consider "saving" one of your best examples for the conclusion. Ending with a statement of your own thinking will help the paragraph have a sense of finality.

Sample Student Work: Conclusion Paragraph

Although numerous religious groups think that the HPV vaccine will cause girls to be sexually active at an earlier age, that view is being challenged by sociologists who say that by 2020, they will have statistics that prove otherwise. Religious groups claim that they will do their own research on the sexual habits of young women who have not received the vaccination. Robert Ainsworth, a behavior scientist and researcher at Yale University, maintains that both groups will undoubtedly have to put controls in place for the ethnicity, socioeconomic status, age, etc, in order to get accurate results in their surveys because the age that a young woman becomes sexually active is usually determined by cultural factors. It is clear that in years to come, we will have more information on this controversial vaccination and the potential effects it will have on women. Five year old girls entering kindergarten receive vaccinations for mumps, measles, and the flu, among others. Will the HPV vaccine soon be next?

Questions for Discussion

1. Examine the sample conclusion paragraph above. What strategy or strategies is the student using? Is this an effective way to end an essay? Why or why not?

2. Based on your writing process, what have you found out about yourself **as a writer** and as a **student**?

    -   Did the "shitty first draft" assignment help your process? Why or why not?
    -   Did you create an outline? Did it work well for you? Why or why not?
    -   Did writing the essay many days before the due date help? Why or why not?
    -   Did the essay change dramatically over the course of the process? How so? And why?
    -   Did you get someone to proof read the essay? Did they help you? Why or why not?
    -   Or, did you proofread the essay? How did you go about it? Do you think it worked well?

CHAPTER 3

You are a Better *Researcher* than You Realize

Research sounds pretty straight forward, right? You type in a couple of key words in a search engine or at the library, find some sources that work for your topic, and done! This oversimplification of the research process is what leads many students to finding sources that are inadequate or even unreliable. Research, like writing, is a process, a term that implies multiple steps.

Take a look at the word "research" and break it down. The prefix "re" is Latin for "again and again" and the word "search" means to seek something by looking thoroughly. In order to perform proper research, students should perform many searches in order seek out the best and most reliable information on their topic. Researching effectively and efficiently is a skill to be learned. In fact, there is a degree dedicated to research skills, a degree in library science. Librarians are expert researchers, but with practice, undergraduate students can learn to be excellent researchers. The following chapter will hopefully teach you to hone those vital research skills, and ultimately help you to become a successful writer.

Exploring the Library

Unfortunately, students hesitate to even go inside the library, let alone check out a book. But as stated earlier, it is a friendly place, with librarians (or professional researchers, as I like to call them) who are itching to help you with your research process. Every library is organized differently, so you just need to go in and explore. Ask the front desk who can help you find sources on your topic. Bring in the essay's assignment sheet to help the librarian better understand your goals.

Scholarly Sources: Written by the Experts

If you are lucky enough to be a college or university student, then you have access to the best resources available! University libraries are where the best sources can be found. Experts in their field, often referred to as scholars, publish their findings and ideas in books and articles which are stored in the library and on the library's online databases.

Did you know that the very professors at your university or college often do research as a part of their job? They are paid to do research in their area of expertise, which we can use to better inform us about the world. College students have access to all of this research! Once you leave college, you will be limited to what is in the public library or free resources online. Your university's library pays for access to academic journals and books, so take advantage of these scholars' work.

What is even better about this body of work, is that often academic articles and books are peer-reviewed, or as we refer to these sources in academia—**scholarly sources**. These are the best, most accurate, and most thorough sources that you can find because a group of researchers who have the same area of expertise review the source carefully and approve it for publication. The author's *peers review* the source, making it even more reliable and trustworthy.

If you are struggling to find good sources, just remember the prefix "re" in "research," which means "again." You must do many searches, many different ways, to find what you need.

Although scholarly sources are the best, other good sources are .gov and .edu websites. Acceptable sources of information are sites like ask.com or about.com. These are good places to get basic information on a topic. You can use these sites to find search terms to find scholarly sources.

Generally poor sources are blogs or personal websites. You can read and get inspiration from these sources, but their authors may lack the credibility that you are looking for.

Finding Sources: You Can Find Sources on Your Topic

Your teacher might assign something called an "Annotated Bibliography," which can be useful to students looking to improve their research skills. This common practice can also allow you to learn to effectively summarize, paraphrase, interpret, and evaluate sources. These skills are each essential in students becoming successful writers. Before getting into how to find sources, let us first define the term "Annotated Bibliography." The noun "annotation" can be defined as a comment or note on some text, and "bibliography" is a list of sources, whether web or print. An "Annotated Bibliography" is a set of source citations with your comments included.

Before you dive into the research process, you may want to brainstorm a bit...

Writing Prompt

Do some focused freewriting on your topic, and see what inspires you. Freewriting will allow you to see what interests you. Next, write down a list of ten different search terms or phrases that you think could be useful. Pay attention to your word choice and its implications on your search results.

Sample Search Queries

The first step in completing this kind of assignment is to locate a source worth annotating. Let's say that your teacher gives you the following topic to research: "health issues correlated with the consumption of dairy milk." You hop online to your library databases and select the popular, "Academic Search Complete" or even "Ebscohost." In the search box, you type in the exact topic that the teacher assigned.

The results are scattered and abundant, to say the least. Your search actually returned NO results, but the computer was able to generate 47,676 based on some of the keywords you typed in.

Here is a sampling of what the database gave you:

"Selected individual differences as predictors of milk production consumption in a group of perimeno-pausal women in the light of health hazards"

"Effects of Milk Type and Consumer Factors on the Acceptance of Milk among Korean Female Consumers"

"Association between Milk and Milk Product Consumption and Anthropemetric Meaures in Adult Men and Women in India: A Cross-Sectional Study"

"Dairy products consumption and calcium intakes of Chinese urban adolescent girls."

How long do you think it would take to sort through 47,676 sources? Days? Weeks? That many search results are actually useless to you. You don't have that kind of time! Not to mention, most of the results are not useful to you. You couldn't possibly make a claim about milk using studies that took place in Korea, India, and China. The cultural practices, diet, etc., are so different in those two countries that the results are probably dramatically different, and thus not helpful to you. That kind of searching isn't efficient.

Let's try again, this time with fewer words, and we can limit the amount and kind of words per search box.

In the first search box, type in "Milk" and select "Title" from the dropdown menu. It's a good bet that a relevant article will have that word in the title. Milk should be the primary subject for it to be useful to you. "Dairy Milk" might also be a useful set of words, but you want to limit the number of words as much as possible. If you get a few articles on other kinds of milk, like soy or goat, then you can easily eliminate them.

In the second search box, type in "Consumption." This word is definitely important, as you wouldn't want to find articles on milk's properties or uses, but instead on the effect of human consumption. In the drop down menu, you select "Abstract," which is a summary of the article. If we were to select "All Text," for instance, then we would get thousands more results. If that term is used even once throughout the article, it would be shown in our results, even if the "consumption" wasn't milk. Since the abstract is much shorter. If the word "consumption" appears there, it's a good chance that milk consumption is the article's central theme.

In the third search box, type in "United States." After seeing multiple articles on milk consumption from around the world, it's a good idea to limit your search to one country. For this drop down menu, you select "All Text" since it is unlikely that the country name would be in the title and while it might be in the summary, having it somewhere in the article's text is likely.

You click "search" and see that 156 results were found! That is a manageable, yet ample amount of results that can be easily sifted through.

The skill of manipulating the library databases to give you your desired result is one that you will learn over time. It is important to understand that search engines like these are sophisticated, but tailored to researchers, not necessarily the public. If you were to type in our initial search query, "health issues correlated with the consumption of dairy milk," into Google, for instance, you may actually get some informative and easy to read results. However, you would also get very few (if any) scholarly or highly detailed sources in that search.

Reading and synthesizing scholarly sources is vital to becoming a sophisticated writer, so while websites like Google may help you with brainstorming, heading to the library or library databases will give you results with more depth, and you can almost guarantee that they will be reliable.

Students often find themselves heading to Google to begin their research process, which is a fine way to start, but your search certainly shouldn't stop there. In fact, Google can help you to find out *what* to type in to those library search databases. For instance, searching for the health issues associated with milk consumption might lead you to a Wikipedia page on prenatal health for pregnant women. You begin to see that obstetricians are researching and conversing about the impact of dairy milk on a fetus. Experts in the field are conversing about this particular issue, telling you that it's worth researching; you go forward and include terms related to pregnancy in your next library database search.

Credible Versus Non-Credible Sources

Even though Wikipedia can be useful, like in the aforementioned scenario, you would never want to use Wikipedia page as a source to cite in any academic work. The information on Wikipedia can easily be modified by anyone browsing the internet, but it will give you a general idea of what to look for while using more sophisticated search engines like Academic Search Complete.

Even the creator of Wikipedia agrees. Take a look at this brief article found in *The Chronicle of Higher Education* published on June 12, 2006:

Reading Critically: "Wikipedia Founder Discourages Academic Use of His Creation"

By Jeffery R. Young

Wikipedia, an online encyclopedia compiled by a distributed network of volunteers, has often come under attack by academics as being shoddy and full of inaccuracies. Even Wikipedia's founder, Jimmy Wales, says he wants to get the message out to college students that they shouldn't use it for class projects or serious research.

Speaking at a conference at the University of Pennsylvania on Friday called "The Hyperlinked Society," Mr. Wales said that he gets about 10 e-mail messages a week from students who complain that Wikipedia has gotten them into academic hot water. "They say, 'Please help me. I got an F on my paper because I cited Wikipedia'" and the information turned out to be wrong, he says. But he said he has no sympathy for their plight, noting that he thinks to himself: "For God sake, you're in college; don't cite the encyclopedia."

Mr. Wales said that leaders of Wikipedia have considered putting together a fact sheet that professors could give out to students explaining what Wikipedia is and that it is not always a definitive source. "It is pretty good, but you have to be careful with it," he said. "It's good enough knowledge, depending on what your purpose is."

In an interview, Mr. Wales said that Wikipedia is ideal for many uses. If you are reading a novel that mentions the Battle of the Bulge, for instance, you could use Wikipedia to get a quick basic overview of the historical event to understand the context. But students writing a paper about the battle should hit the history books.

How to Spot a Credible Source

Once you start to find sources, you need to decide if the source is any good, or to be more specific, is the source **credible?**

For each source that you find, answer the following questions. The answers to these questions will help you decide if the source is a credible, good source.

1.   What is the title of the article or book?

2.   How did you find the source? Using the library's online databases? Asking a librarian? The card catalogue?

3.   What is the name of the journal if it is an article or the publisher if it is a book?

4.   Who is the intended audience of this source? How do you know?

5.   Who is the author? What are his or her credentials? Do these credentials make the author qualified to write on this issue in your opinion?

6.   In a single sentence, state the main idea and purpose of the source. To persuade? Inform? Entertain? Bring awareness? Etc.

How to Avoid Research Fatigue

Much like writing that first draft, research fatigue happens to even the most seasoned students and scholars. We stare at our computer or sit staring at the shelves in the library. We have been researching for awhile. We see a title that seems interesting, so we make a note of it. We see another source that looks decent, and we print it out. You start to run out of steam pretty quickly.

You may be finding sources quickly, but you soon become overwhelmed with the vast amount of information out there. You soon get tired and maybe bored. This is research fatigue, and here is how you may be able to avoid it.

First of all, don't limit yourself to the library for research. When your riding the bus to class, for instance, pull up the library's databases on your mobile device. Do a couple of searches there if you feel inspired. Most databases have an option to email yourself the file, complete with a perfectly formatted citation. This convenience can save you time; plus doing research often in small time frames is more manageable than sitting down for hours at a time.

Second, if you are at the library or at home while researching, take your time. The *quality* of your sources is more important than the *quantity*. If you find a good source, don't just print it and continue searching! Hang with it for a minute. Read the abstract (a summary of the source written by it's author). If you still think that it will be useful, then consider printing it. As stated earlier, many databased have an option to print a citation with the source, so take advantage of that convenience. If the database doesn't have that option, or you found the source on a website, then immediately make a note of the author, the title, and the date that you found it. If you don't do this now, it will be difficult to track the source down later.

Continue to work with the source. Read through it at least once, highlighting or underlining what you think is important or useful. While you read, evaluate the source for credibility. Does the author seem biased? Do a quick internet search of the author. Is he or she qualified to write on this topic? Have they written on it before? Are they associated with an organization or university that may represent a bias? For instance, if the article is on women's reproductive rights, and the author is a professor from a Catholic University, that will change the way you read the article. Conversely, if the article is on the unborn's right to life, and the author is a professor at a public university, that may also influence the content. Make notes on the source where you notice that a bias may be present.

Remember, a totally non-biased source simply doesn't exist! Sources aren't written in a vacuum. They are written by a human being with a unique set of experiences during a unique place in time. Once you have a good idea of the content of the source, the credibility and biases of the author, and have made a note of the citation, then you can continue to search for more.

Doing a bit of work on the front-end will save you from research fatigue later on!

Writing a Research Proposal

Writing a research proposal can help students stay focused as they locate sources and begin the writing process. Essentially, students will write on what they propose for their research and writing process. Research proposals (similar to introduction paragraphs) often begin with broader, contextual information, and they often end with more specific, concrete information.

The most common error when writing a research proposal is to begin *too broad.* For instance, you wouldn't want to start with "Since the beginning of time...." or "The world is a complicated place..." or even "There are many controversies in our society..." Those phrases have little meaning. Instead of going *that* broad, think about writing broad information *on the topic* itself.

Another common mistake for these proposals is not being specific *enough* towards the end. Concrete examples, anecdotes, etc., can make the proposal engaging. This bit of specific information can help to illustrate what you will do in your future essay.

Sample Student Work: Research Proposal

Research Proposal:

Considering Whether Employers Should Look at Potential Employees' Social Media Profiles

The World Wide Web has been a place for communication since its introduction in the 1990s. Before long, websites dedicated to online socializing came on the scene. In the early 2000s, MySpace was the most popular social networking website. Millions of mostly teenaged people came together to create a personal profile and communicate with friends. Unbeknownst to its users and the public, this was the beginning of the social media era that we know today. MySpace was soon taken over by (now) most popular social media website in the world, Facebook. Originally a place where college students could indicate that they were looking for either "friendship" or a "relationship," Facebook is now open to the public who use it for everything from advertising their small business, sharing photos of their dinner, to criticizing presidential candidates. As one can see from this very brief history, the function of social media has morphed from users socializing to users forging a comprehensive online personal identity. What we post on various social media networks becomes our public identity, whether we like it or not.

This online identity is available for the world to see, even if you think that your profile is "private." Comprehensive social media profiles have become useful tools for not only networking and socializing, but for sharing in general. This excessive sharing can often backfire on users. Police check the social media sites of suspected criminals, and often catch them in the act due to the "instant" updates that users often provide. But social media profiles have also become problematic for users in a potentially unfair way. For instance, employers can use social media sites to check up on their employees in ways that users deem unfairly invasive. A recent news story detailed the story of a teacher at a private Christian high school who posted photos on Instagram in which she is shown drinking wine with friends. She was fired by the school, who claimed that she is not a good example for the students and her hobbies are not in line with the school's Christian mission statement. The ethics of an employer using social media sites to investigate their employees is the focus of my research. Some of the questions I will answer are: should an employee's personal life be considered in their job performance evaluations? Why do employers deem this appropriate? Are there any jobs or circumstances in which this investigating might be necessary? What can employees do to protect themselves and their job security? What can employers lawfully do if they have reason to believe that an employee's personal life portrayed online is impacting their job? The answers to these questions will help me develop a more informed opinion on this controversial issue.

Annotating Your Sources: Unlocking your Understanding

Annotating sources is not a useless activity although it can seem like it at the time! Annotating sources is a good idea because it allows students to actually *use* the source later on in research paper, for instance. Creating an annotated bibliography is merely another step in the writing process. The goals of this kind of activity are to sharpen your critical thinking skills by reading sophisticated, scholarly sources, learn to paraphrase and summarize accurately and easily, and to locate reliable, credible sources.

To "annotate" means to add notes or comment to a source. A "bibliography" is a list of sources referenced. An "annotated bibliography" is a list of sources with their accompanying notes. The best and most useful way to write an annotated bibliography is to do three things with each source:

1. Position
2. Summarize
3. Evaluate

Positioning the Text: Considering Context

Positioning the text is the first step that students most often forget, yet it may be the most important of all. In order to best understand the text as a source, we must first position it in a particular time and space. We must put the source into *context*. You may want to ask yourself these questions in order to position the text accurately: who is the author or publisher? What do you know about him or her? Is he or she qualified to write on this issue? What are the author's potential biases? Whose interests does the source represent? To what audience is the message directed?

For example, let's say that you are writing an essay on potentially lowering the drinking age in the United States from 21 to 18. You will find a variety of sources on this issue. Many may take similar positions and give similar reasons for their claims, but the difference is that they all have a different position in time, space, and authorship.

Let's take a look at this source: http://www.madd.org/blog/2014/march/lowering-the-drinking-age-is.html

Reading Critically: Lowering the Drinking Age is Not the Answer

By MADD   March 21, 2014

At MADD, we support the 21 Minimum Legal Drinking Age (MLDA) because it saves lives, prevents injuries, and protects still-developing brains. That's not to say that underage drinking doesn't still happen, but rather that we need to focus on ways to improve education and enforcement of the existing law—not try to change it.

In a recent CNN.com opinion piece about lowering the drinking age to 19, the author asserts that the 21 MLDA is a "national joke." However, MADD believes that it's not funny, and it's only a joke if we choose to let it be one.

Underage drinking is as much a youth problem as it is an adult problem. And when we're talking about college campuses, it's true that some administrators are turning a blind eye to the problem. But that doesn't mean we shouldn't strive to do what we know is best for our youth.

Perhaps the issue is one of complacency. We as a nation shouldn't assume that teen alcohol use is a rite of passage. Instead, we need to agree that 4,700 deaths each year is unacceptable, and do something about it. We can start by setting rules and expectations at home, and then supporting enforcement of existing laws and consequences.

Underage drinking should not be a foregone conclusion. We owe it to our kids and to their futures to do everything in our power to keep them healthy and safe.

The research is clear that the 21 MLDA saves lives—and that science trumps personal opinion. We're past the point of a debate on the 21 MLDA.

MADD has always, and will continue to support the 21 MLDA because our kids are worth it.

In order to position this text in the rhetorical situation, we need to examine the author. The author of this brief article is MADD, or Mothers Against Drunk Driving. According to their website, this organization was "Founded by a mother whose daughter was killed by a drunk driver, Mothers Against Drunk Driving® (MADD) is the nation's largest nonprofit working to protect families from drunk driving and underage drinking."

Understanding the goals of this organization better positions the article for the reader. We can see that the founders and members of this organization are particularly sensitive to the dangers of alcohol; therefore, they would be staunchly against not only drunk driving, but also allowing any extra access to alcohol whatsoever. This bias impacts their argument. In the rhetorical situation, we can see that the author has impacted the message.

If we position the text in time, we can see that this article comes as a response to the CNN.com article, which is referenced in the MADD article. With a bit of research, one can see that the CNN.com article was published just one day prior to the MADD article. The CNN article, found here: http://www.cnn.com/2014/03/20/opinion/cohan-underage-drinking-duke/ is below:

Reading Critically: *Get Real, Lower the Drinking Age to 19*

By: William Cohan   March 20, 2014

It's been eight years since a black exotic dancer in Durham, North Carolina, accused three white Duke University lacrosse players of rape, sexual assault and kidnapping at a party. Whether you believe justice was adequately served—without a trial, the North Carolina attorney general unilaterally declared the indicted players innocent—one fact remains indisputable: a whole lot of underage drinking of beer and Jack Daniels was going on throughout much of that March day, badly impairing the judgment of the more than 40 man-boys in attendance.

According to a June 2006 study by Aaron White, then an assistant professor at the Duke University Medical Center, about 40% of college freshmen admitted they engaged in binge drinking: five or more drinks on one occasion. Some 20% of college freshmen admitted they drank even more: between 10 and 15 drinks per drinking session.

"College students drink at levels far higher than we expected," White wrote in the report. "We found that roughly 20% of all freshmen males had 10 or more drinks at least once during the two-week period (of the study.) This is twice the binge threshold." He found that "highly excessive drinking" is more common on American college campuses than in other countries, although in Denmark, Great Britain, Australia, New Zealand, South Africa and Russia there are also high rates of drinking on college campuses.

College and university presidents generally agree that binge and underage drinking are the single greatest problems facing their schools, in large part because of all the bad behavior—including rape—that results from excessive and acute drinking on campus.

Not surprisingly, Duke students are hardly immune to the epidemic of excessive drinking. In its own 2000 study about alcohol abuse among its students, Duke found that 41% said they engaged in binge drinking. In the first two months of the 2000 school year—Duke's 75th anniversary—18 students were admitted to the emergency room with alcohol-related problems, 13 of whom were freshmen.

Despite the drinking age of 21, about 74% of drinking violations at Duke in 1999 were committed by freshmen. James Clack, a student affairs administrator, wrote a message to incoming freshmen in August 2000 telling them not to be pressured "to become a dangerous drinker. . . . If you want to major in alcohol, please go elsewhere."

Clack's admonition fell, and continues to fall, on deaf ears. Not only did excessive drinking lead to the lacrosse players' decision to hire, at a cost of $400 each, the two strippers in the first place—apparently not uncommon at Duke fraternity and sorority parties—but it also led to the boys' taunting of the women with a broomstick, to their unsavory public humiliation of the two dancers as the sexual fervor in the living room ratcheted up and to their hurling of ugly racial epithets at them after they abruptly left the off-campus house.

Whether it also led the three indicted players to rape Crystal Mangum, as she said happened in one of the bathrooms, will never be known. But while the debate about that continues, the open question remains of how much longer we as a nation are going to continue to tolerate underage drinking on college campuses.

The drinking age of 21 is a national joke. Every college campus in the country is filled with students who violate the drinking law every week, if not every day, while university administrators turn a mostly blind eye.

Some matriculating freshmen know intuitively that soon after the acceptance letter arrives, the next task is to obtain—usually for around $100 or so—a spiffy fake identification card that will convince inquiring minds that its holder can drink legally. And the IDs are pretty darn convincing.

But it's all a farce, and does nobody any favors. For any semblance of hope that binge drinking, and its attendant bad behavior, can be curtailed on college campuses, Congress must act sooner rather than later to lower the drinking age to 19 years old.

That seems to me, as the father of two underage college students, the right age for drinking to be legal. By then, when most students are sophomores, one year of college will be in the bag, with the awkward but necessary social adjustments mostly accomplished. Instead of students continuously lusting after the forbidden fruit of alcohol and sneaking around furtively with bottles of vodka and rum and then quickly guzzling them in an effort to get limbered up to be able to "hook up" with one's peers, perhaps a more, shall we say, refined and responsible approach to alcohol can prevail on campus.

A drinking age of 19 would also mean that easily three-quarters of the students on a college campus would no longer be violating the law by either drinking on campus or in unsupervised homes off-campus.

The crimes allegedly committed by the three Duke lacrosse players happened in a house off Duke's East Campus. Needless to say, these off-campus binge parlors are not popular in the neighborhood.

Of course, along with a lowering of the drinking age to 19, a zero tolerance policy must be put in place for anything approaching driving while intoxicated. In Brazil, for instance, it is illegal to drive with even a trace amount of alcohol in the bloodstream; in the United States, the 0.08% threshold should be abandoned in favor of zero tolerance. Anyone caught driving with any amount of alcohol in their bloodstream should have his or her driving privileges suspended for at least three years.

In October 2005, Duke President Richard Brodhead gave an interview to the National Public Radio station in Chapel Hill. The night of the March 13, 2006, party was still six months in the future. But the residents of the Durham neighborhood where student partying had ratcheted up exponentially over the previous years were already in open revolt. They were sick of underage drinking, the late-night noise, the public urination and the intimidating presence in their midst of large groups of thoroughly inebriated college students. They had asked the Duke administration and the Durham police to begin cracking down on the drunken and lewd behavior.

This came up during Brodhead's interview. One of the original signatories of the Amethyst Initiative—a group that advocates lowering the drinking age to 18 and encouraging a debate among students, faculty and administrators about the responsible role of alcohol on campus—Brodhead has long been working to confront head-on the drinking problem on campuses.

From his answers on public radio, it was obvious Brodhead knew he was sitting on a powder keg. "The problem of drinking in college, the problem of rowdiness in college—this is by no means a Duke problem," he said. "It's a problem that all of us face."

One caller to the show—Betty, a resident of the Durham neighborhood where the lacrosse team would soon have its fateful party—asked Brodhead to comment on her perception that the students seemed to be regularly drinking to excess and then causing trouble. Brodhead said "It's a challenge for everybody, and we can't make the problem go away by wishing it didn't exist."

Continuing to pretend that underage binge drinking on college campuses and the horrific behavior that derives from it doesn't exist is not a responsible and mature response to an obvious systemic problem.

We can't continue to anesthetize ourselves. One possible solution is to lower the drinking age to 19 and to enact a zero tolerance policy for drinking and driving. There are undoubtedly others. Let's solve this.

If we position this source, we will find out that the author, William Cohan, is also a business man and book author. In fact, he wrote the book, *The Price of Silence: The Duke Lacrosse Scandal, the Power of the Elite, and the Corruption of our Great Universities,* which details the scandal at Duke as well as other instances of sexual misconduct and excessive drinking that occur at universities around the country. He mentions this scandal in his article, but with this bit of knowledge, we discover that the author is actually much closer to the issue of underage drinking than your average CNN.com journalist. He has done extensive research and investigating into this very issue.

Now that we have information about the authors of these sources, we are able to effectively position them as sources in the rhetorical situation. Their experiences as human beings with the issues of drunk driving have informed their opinions, and thus these sources.

Summarizing and Paraphrasing: Two Vital Tools

The next step after positioning the text is to **summarize** the source. While this step may seem straightforward enough, it can often be the trickiest one. It's up to you to represent the source's message accurately, in just a few lines. Students often confuse summarizing with paraphrasing, and this can lead to frustration or anxiety about the writing process. The key to avoid getting overwhelmed by your sources and the writing process in general is understanding how to summarize and paraphrase accurately and efficiently.

Paraphrasing is putting the source in your own words, into your own language that you feel comfortable with, only you might condense it slightly. Paraphrasing a source allows you to actually use it! When you completely understand the source, you will be able to integrate it into your essay (or summarize it if you're writing an annotated bibliography). A paraphrase includes more details than a summary.

Summarizing, on the other hand, is much shorter than the original source material. You are putting the main idea of the source into your own words, into your own language. A summary might only be a few lines. A good annotation will include a complete summary of the source as well as a brief paraphrase of any pertinent material.

These two tools, paraphrasing and summarizing, will allow you to understand your source material, as well as better communicate your own ideas.

NOTE: Quoting a source is another way to convey its important points. Only about 10% of your essay should be directly quoted material. Only quote a source if you think there is no possible way to say it more clearly or concisely. More on quotations in Chapter 5. Don't forget that you must cite a paraphrase, summary, or quote. If it's not your idea, then you must give credit to whoever did come up with it. If it's common knowledge or a universally held truth, then there is no need to cite that.

Paraphrase and Summary Practice

The following excerpt is taken from Kosuke Koyoma's article titled *A Theological Reflection on Religious Pluralism*.

> We live today in a world that is religiously and morally pluralistic. According to one recent reference book, religious pluralism is "the view that different or even contradictory, forms of religious belief and behaviour could or even should coexist. The problem with religious pluralism arises when one particular tradition (the mainstream) dominates society, denying the legitimacy of other streams and marginalizing them as sectarian phenomena."
>
> Stanley J. Samartha writes, "Pluralism does not relativize Truth. It relativizes different responses to Truth which are conditioned by history and culture. It rejects the claim of any particular response to be absolute."[2] The acknowledgment that no one can hold the truth in the palm of his or her hand is the basic orientation of sound religious pluralism. Truth is not identical with our truth claims.
>
> In a pluralistic world, those who embrace a particular position must be enlightened about positions other than their own. It takes critical intellectual effort to understand and appreciate the plural reality of truths and their meaningful coexistence. There are Hindu, Buddhist, Taoist, Confucian, Jewish, Christian and Islamic religious experiences and expressions that inform respective truth perceptions. This challenges the conviction of "no other name" (Acts 4:12) which has guided Christian theology for centuries. It is a worthy and serious challenge.
>
> Koyama, K. (1999), A Theological Reflection on Religious Pluralism.
The Ecumenical Review, 51: 160–171.

Sample Student Work

Below is a student's attempt to paraphrase the first paragraph of the excerpt above:

Kosuke Koyama, the author of *A Theological Reflection on Religious Pluralism*, states that we currently live in a religious pluralistic society. He defines this term as the view that many different religions can or maybe should exist all at once. The author admits that religious pluralism becomes problematic when one religion dominates society and claims that all other less common religions are not legitimate and therefore exist only to contrast the mainstream.

Paraphrasing Exercise

Try paraphrasing the second half of the passage yourself. Here it is again, for your reference, with space for notes below each section:

> Stanley J. Samartha writes, "Pluralism does not relativize Truth. It relativizes different responses to Truth which are conditioned by history and culture. It rejects the claim of any particular response to be absolute."[2] The acknowledgment that no one can hold the truth in the palm of his or her hand is the basic orientation of sound religious pluralism. Truth is not identical with our truth claims.

NOTES:

_____

_____

Final Paraphrase:

_____

_____

_____

_____

_____

_____

_____

_____

_____

_____

_____

In a pluralistic world, those who embrace a particular position must be enlightened about positions other than their own. It takes critical intellectual effort to understand and appreciate the plural reality of truths and their meaningful coexistence. There are Hindu, Buddhist, Taoist, Confucian, Jewish, Christian and Islamic religious experiences and expressions that inform respective truth perceptions. This challenges the conviction of "no other name" (Acts 4:12) which has guided Christian theology for centuries. It is a worthy and serious challenge.

NOTES:

_____

_____

Final Paraphrase:

_____

_____

_____

_____

_____

_____

Now, try summarizing the entire passage in just a couple of brief sentences:

_____

_____

_____

_____

_____

_____

Questions for Discussion

1. Reflect on your paraphrasing and summarizing skills.

2. What is the most difficult part of paraphrasing and/or summarizing a source?

3. How did you go about paraphrasing in the previous activity? Would you change your strategy in the future?

4. What was the easiest part for you? How could you improve in the future?

Evaluate the Source: Is it Actually Useful to You?

Deciding whether or not the source was any good in general was described earlier,, but you can also decide whether or not the source is actually useful for your purposes. For instance, is this information already discussed in another one of your sources? Well, then in may not be useful to you. But if the source takes an alternative position on a topic, then that is a good one to hold on to.

At this stage, you will also want to think about how and where you will use the source. If you read a telling anecdote or narrative in a source, make a note that this may be useful in the introduction of your essay, for instance. If you see a source chock full of expert testimony, make a note that this source can be used as evidence to support your claim.

Annotated Bibliography Peer Revision

Peer revision is a very useful tool for both the author and the reader. Not only does the author receive valuable feedback on their work, but the reader can see a new way of writing an essay and thinking about an issue.

STEP ONE—Evaluating for Content: As you read your partner's draft, think about the following questions that reference CONTENT.

Are the sources not only reliable, but also diverse? Meaning, do they represent a variety of points of view and purposes? And do they come from the library databases or just the web?

Do the annotations position the text and discuss the author and/or publication adequately?

Do the annotations summarize the text adequately? Meaning, does it make the author's main point(s) clear? And does it explicitly state what conclusions the author comes to? Does it seem well-developed, or does something seem missing?

Do the annotations evaluate the text as a source and explain how or why it may or may not be useful? Does the annotation reference the text in a rhetorical way?

Write your partner a note about what he or she did well and what he or she could still work on to improve the project in terms of CONTENT. Use the questions above as a guide.

STEP TWO—Evaluating for Style: As you read your partner's draft, think about the following questions that reference STYLE.

Does the format of the annotations follow the instructions laid out on the assignment sheet? (Single spaced, Times New Roman font, citations before each annotation, etc.)

Does the citation look like it is in MLA format?

Are the annotations overly wordy? Or overly vague?

Does your partner make clear "whose idea" each point is? (They should make it clear that these are the author's thoughts, not their own.)

Are quotes dropped in, or are they contextualized accurately?

Write your partner a note about what he or she did well and what he or she could still work on to improve the project in terms of STYLE. Use the questions above as a guide.

STEP THREE—Feedback Discussion: After reading and evaluating your partner's work, give them their draft back and also give them your notes to use during revision. After giving him or her some time to read over your comments, have a discussion that might clarify or further enhance your written comments.

Questions for Discussion

Reflect on your research process. Write a detailed, thoughtful paragraph describing what you found out about yourself as a researcher and learner. Use the following questions to guide your answer:

1. Are you still interested in the topic you chose?
2. How did your topic change during the research process?
3. What did you find easiest and most difficult about the process?
4. How did you stay organized (or unorganized) while finding, reading, and writing about your sources?
5. How will you modify your research strategies in the future?

CHAPTER 4

You are a Better *Analytical Thinker* than You Realize

Once we learn research skills, learning how to think about our sources in an analytical way is the next step in becoming the best academic writer that you can be. Analyzing issues, topics, or a visual or written text will allow you to develop your critical thinking skills, thus making your writing skills richer and more interesting in content.

Analysis skills are actually quite intuitive if students can understand how s l o w the process of critical thinking really is. Slowing down and examining the words and sentences, not just thinking about the main idea, is how we begin the analytical thinking process.

In their 1982 book, *From Speaking of Words: A Language Reader,* Genevieve and Newman Birk teach students how to examine words and sentences in an analytical way. In the aforementioned book, they have a chapter entitled, "Selection, Slanting, and Charged Language." The concepts covered in this chapter are very useful for students who want to learn to analyze any given concept or item, particularly when it comes to language and words.

Understanding Birks' concepts on language will allow you to become an expert "analyzer." Some of these concepts include:

1. **The Principle of Selection**
2. **The Principle of Slanting**
3. **The Principle of Slanting by use of Charge Language**

The Principle of Selection

Every person has their own unique principal of selection. Our minds can consciously or unconsciously select what facts to take in. We couldn't possibly notice everything about an environment or piece of literature, for instance, so our minds only absorb some of it. Our principal of selection determines what our mind notices. This principal will take shape depending on a whole host of characteristics: our gender, race, sexuality, age, and socio-economic status, among others.

Adapted from: *Speaking of Words: A Language Reader* by Genevieve and Newman Birk.

In their book, the Birks give us the following example to better illustrate this concept. If a lumberjack, an artist, and a tree surgeon are all observing a tree, will what each notice be different? Of course. Each has their own principal of selection, so their observations will vary.

Questions for Discussion

1. Using the Birks' principal of selection, what would the lumberjack notice about the tree?
2. The artist?
3. The tree surgeon?

Applying The Principle of Selection

As stated earlier, all people have their own principal of selection, and that includes authors, experts, and journalists who we typically trust. As you sort through your research and begin to analyze sources, keep in mind that the article or book you're reading was written by a human being with his or her own set of selection patterns that will impact how he or she writes. Whatever words you read have been filtered by their principal of selection. Whether consciously or unconsciously, what the author chooses to write has been shaped in some way.

Acknowledging that we all select a different set of items to notice will help you to see scholars not as truth-tellers but instead as human beings who come from a particular culture from a particular point in time from a particular set of circumstances.

When you are reading, remember that you too have a predisposition to notice particular words or concepts more than others due to your own selection patterns. Attempting to become aware of your subconscious thought processes during the writing process will bring your biases to the forefront. Try not to get anxious about your biases. Everyone has them, and they impact everyone every single day.

It's important to reflect on this because being cognizant of your own biases and weaknesses both as a human being and as a student writer will make your writing come much easier.

Partner Activity

Select a partner and together, take a look at the image below. For 60 seconds only, write down everything that you notice about the ad. After 60 seconds, compare you and your partner's lists. What differences and similarities do you see? Based on "The Principal of Selection," why do these differences and similarities exist? Consider you and your partner's different interests, experiences, and personal, cultural, and social differences during your discussion.

© Teddy Leung/Shutterstock.com

The Principle of Slanting

A second concept from the Birks' book is the "The Principle of Slanting," an action that occurs after our minds select facts. We must express that knowledge into words, which will be *slanted* based on our unique human characteristics.

The Birks' define slanting as "the process of selecting (1) knowledge—factual and attitudinal; (2) words; and (3) emphasis, to achieve the intention of the communicator."

All communication is slanted in some way, and there are three main types of slanting: favorable, unfavorable, and balanced. One can slant in a variety of ways: through emphasis, selection of facts, and charged language.

Slanting by Use of Emphasis

An author can slant by use of emphasis by stressing particular words or groups of words to make them seem more or less important. One way to emphasize words is to **bold** or *italicize* them, for instance. The author could use capital letters, underlines, exclamation points, etc., to slant their communication. Connective words and the order of words are other ways to slant through emphasis and shape the reader's perception of the subject at hand.

Take a look at the examples below and decide if the sentences are **favorable, unfavorable,** or **balanced**.

He is intelligent and boastful.   He is boastful and intelligent.

He is intelligent yet boastful.   He is boastful yet intelligent.

Even though he is boastful, he is intelligent.   Even though he is boastful, he is intelligent.

Slanting by Use of Charged Words

Another way to slant communication is through the use of positive or negative charged words. Two words may have similar meanings, but one could be positively charged and one could be negatively charged, giving the reader a particular impression. See the example sentences below.

Positively Charged Language: She is a **critical** thinker.

Negatively Charged Language: She is a **judgmental** person.

Partner Activity

Read the passages below, placing a "+" over words (or groups of words) that are positively charged and a "-"over words that are negatively charged.

I.   The new kittens purred at their new owner. Their fluffy black fur shined in the morning sunlight, giving the woman a sense of peace. The kittens played enthusiastically, pawing at one another with vigor. As the tiny cats romped around the woman's bedroom, she pondered her future with the new pets.

II.   The new kittens growled at their new owner. Their overgrown fur looked greasy in the glaring light, making the woman feel tired. The kittens played aggressively, scratching one another violently. As the scrawny cats sprinted around the woman's bedroom, she began to dread her future with the new animals.

Individual Activity

Bring a copy of your college's newspaper to class. Select an *opinion* article (like a letter to the editor or personal column), and underline portions that are a) emphasized by order of words, and b) slanted by use of charged language.

Errors in Logic: How to Spot Them

The following is a list of errors in logic, or sometimes called "logical fallacies." You want to avoid these when making your own argument and look for them in others' arguments. Below each definition, you will find an example. In the space provided, explain why the example is an error in logic. Some of these examples sound downright silly, but starting with easy-to-spot fallacies is a good introduction to the more complex arguments that this text will cover later.

Adapted From: Brannan, Bob. A Writer's Workshop: Crafting Paragraphs, Building Essays. 3rd Edition. Boston: McGraw-Hill Higher Education, 2009. Print.

1. **Oversimplifying a complex issue**: This logical fallacy occurs when someone reduces an issue, controversy, or problem to make it appear far simpler than it actually is. They might claim that the issue has only one solution, only two "sides," or they might use words like "simply," "always," "every time," etc., instead of using terms that are more inclusive and allow for possibilities or extenuating circumstances.

   Example: "No one should ever use a gun to hurt another person."

   _____

2. **Overgeneralizing from limited evidence:** This error occurs when someone makes a claim that cannot be supported by the evidence provided. This person draws a conclusion that is overly general.

   Example: "It has been proven that on average, vegetarians have a lower body mass index, so all people should eat a vegetarian diet if they want to be healthy."

   _____

2. **Drawing an unwarranted conclusion**: Similar to the previous logical fallacy, this one also draws a conclusion that is incorrect. Here though, it isn't because the evidence is too broad, but because the evidence simply doesn't prove the claim. Drawing an unwarranted conclusion can often utilize common stereotypes.

   Example: "That woman has a pit bull puppy; I bet she will use him in dog fights. Stay away from her because her dog is dangerous."

   _____

3.   **Confusing time order with cause**: People may incorrectly assume that because a particular event occurs before another, the two are somehow related. An event preceding another does not mean that it was the cause of the second event.

Example: "A black cat once crossed my path right before I got into a fender-bender. I'm steering clear of black cats from now on."

_____

4.   **Using a faulty analogy:** This error in logic occurs when someone uses an invalid comparison to make an argument. The comparison might use a metaphor, simile, etc., and it is invalid because the two things being compared are not actually similar.

Example: "Adopting a puppy is like giving birth to a newborn baby; both are a lot of work and can keep you up at night!"

_____

5.   **Attacking a person, not an argument**: name-calling or attacking the opposition is one way that some people try to win arguments. They believe that attacking or undermining someone else will make them appear to have the better argument, when in actuality, this is a logical fallacy and does not help their case.

Example: "People who don't support alternative energy legislation are greedy and selfish; whoever thinks that we don't need alternative energy sources in this country is insane."

_____

6.   **Running with the crowd**: The herd impulse is a powerful one. Instead of giving good reasons supported with evidence for why an argument is valid, a person may merely discuss how other people agree, and therefore we should too.

Example: "I probably shouldn't drink soda so much, but I know a lot of older people who drink soda a lot, and they seem healthy, so I'm sure its OK."

_____

7.   **Correlation equals causation:** Just because two things are correlated, or coincide, does not mean that they are causal, or caused by the other.

Example: The image below is a bowl of multi-grain cereal. Read the text and explain how it is a logical fallacy.

Example: "People who eat multi-grains tend to weigh less than people who do not. Eating multi-grain cereals can help you to lose weight."

A lot of these logical fallacies probably seem SUPER obvious to you. Like this book revealed early on, you really are a better writer than you realize. If you identified that even a couple of these examples are problematic, then you can rest assured that you are a pretty darn good analytical thinker. Good analytical thinking skills are a vital step in becoming a successful writer in an academic and professional setting, so you are on your way!

Identifying Assumptions

Students often look at the term *assumption* and consider it a word that identifies a mistake. Making assumptions are bad, right? If you don't know for sure or don't have evidence to support, then you shouldn't draw that conclusion. There is another way to look at assumptions though, and they are called **Underlying Assumptions.** This kind of assumption can also be thought of like a universally held truth. You don't need evidence for it because our culture makes the assumption for the sake of time and ease. For instance, right before you open the door to your classroom, you assume that the desks will be lined up and facing the board. Imagine if we didn't ever make assumptions. We would walk into every scenario utterly shocked and surprised!

Assumptions make our lives easier, but they can also prevent us from seeing things clearly. Racism, for instance, involves making assumptions about a particular cultural group. People are racist for all kinds of reasons, but one of them is that it is simply easier. It is easier and faster to assume that all policemen treat minorities with distain or that all politicians are dishonest than to consider all the other options depending on the context or situation. If we make assumptions like these, then we don't have to waste time thinking about all of the other options.

Solve the Riddle

We are all susceptible to making assumptions because we are human. We seek the knowledge that is the easiest to access! This saves us time and effort. Sometimes those assumptions are useful, like the assumption that when your light turns green, the other car will stop. Other assumptions can be harmful or at least prevent us from being open-minded. Or, it could prevent us from solving the riddle below:

> A father and son are in a terrible car accident. The father is killed and the son, critically injured, is rushed into emergency surgery. The surgeon walks into the operating room, looks at the boy's face and says, "I can't operate on this boy; he's my son." How can this be possible?

The proposed solutions to this riddle vary, but the most popular answers are that the boy is adopted or that the boy's parents are in a homosexual relationship. After several minutes, you may have realized that the solution is simple! The surgeon is the boy's mother. Why was that riddle so difficult when the answer was so obvious?

In the United States, we live in a patriarchy, or a culture that is male-dominated and led. We think of authority figures as male, not female, so didn't immediately occur to us that the surgeon could be female. This cultural norm is deeply rooted. Terms like "man of the house," "man up," "you run like a girl," and the fact that the term "career woman" exists and "career man" does not all prove that we live in a patriarchal culture, or at the very least that we view men as working, strong, authoritative. There are loads of female doctors, but since these cultural norms are deeply rooted, we are more likely to see men in an authoritative role. Imagine if the mother in the riddle was a nurse instead of a surgeon, do you think that it would have been solved faster?

There isn't anything wrong with these assumptions per say. We aren't immune to the forces of our culture and media, but it is important to acknowledge that we are susceptible to making assumptions. Once we are aware of that tendency, we can try to see beyond them, giving us a higher level of thinking. This higher level of thinking helps students to communicate more accurately.

Partner Activity

Every advertisement that we see is an abbreviated argument, attempting to convince us to purchase the product or whatever is being sold.

The image below is of the two spokesmen for Old Spice, a company that sells hygiene products for men. The man on the left is Isaiah Mustafa and the man on the right is Fabio Lanzoni. A quick internet search will tell you a lot about them if you're not sure!

© Helga Esteb/Shutterstock.com

What kind of assumption did the company make when they chose these spokesmen? Write your ideas in the space below.

_____

_____

_____

Identifying Contradictions

To put it simply, a contradiction is a statement that denies the truth of another. If an author contradicts him or herself, we can usually spot it fairly quickly. "I eat potato chips with my turkey sandwich every day. I avoid processed food when possible," for instance, is a contradiction because most potato chips, deli meats, and sandwich breads are all highly processed foods.

An **inherent contradiction**, however, is when someone makes an assertion that contradicts with what you, the reader, personally believe to be true. Like this has been explained earlier, we all have a different set of biases and come to an argument or controversy with a different point of view. This isn't necessarily a bad thing, but something to be aware of. When listening to or reading someone else's argument, keep in mind that they too have their own set of circumstances. What they say or write may contradict with what you believe to be true. It doesn't mean that you or the author is right or wrong, but means that an inherent contradiction is present.

Politics is a great place to examine inherent contradictions. Let's look at a woman named Melissa. Melissa considers herself a political conservative. She is pro-life and does not support the right to an abortion. She also believes in the 2nd amendment to the fullest extent; Melissa thinks that all citizens have the right to bear arms for protection and safety.

Another woman named Amy considers herself a political liberal. She is pro-choice and supports the right to an abortion. She believes that the 2nd amendment was written before weapons were as sophisticated as they are now, and guns should largely be outlawed because they kill people.

Question for Discussion

- What do you think that Amy would say is the inherent contradiction in Melissa's argument? What would Melissa say is the inherent contradiction in Amy's argument?

Reading Critically: Wolman's Time to Cash Out: Why Paper Money Hurts the Economy

The following excerpt is from David Wolman's article in *Wired Magazine* entitled "Time to Cash Out: Why Paper Money Hurts the Economy," written in 2009. In general, the author makes a strong argument for going cashless, but some readers may see some logical fallacies, assumptions, or inherent contradictions. Underline the sections which contain the fallacies and in the space following, explain how the selection could be an error in logic, assumption, or contradiction.

"Imagine someday paying for a beer with frequent flier miles. Opponents used to argue that killing cash would hurt low-income workers—for instance, by eliminating cash tips. But a modest increase in the minimum wage would offset that loss; government savings from not printing money could go toward lower taxes for employers. And let's not forget the transaction costs of paper currency, especially for the poor. If you're less well off, check-cashing fees and 10-mile bus rides to make payments or purchases are not trivial. Yes, panhandlers will be out of luck, but to use that as a reason for preserving a costly, outdated technology would be a sad admission, as if tossing spare change is the best we can do for the homeless. Killing currency wouldn't be a trauma; it'd be euthanasia. We have the technology to move to a more efficient, convenient, freely flowing medium of exchange. Emoney is no longer just a matter of geeks playing games."

Ethos, Logos, Pathos: Understanding this Rhetorical Trio

Your teacher might ask you write a rhetorical analysis essay, and while that genre of essay might seem intimidating, it's actually the most fun to write. Before getting into the specifics of this kind of assignment, let's first think about what the terms *rhetorical* and *analysis* actually mean. **Rhetoric** is a noun that refers to the art of using language to communicate something—an argument, a point of view, or even a story. The term *rhetorical*, however, is an adjective that describes something that is used solely for stylistic purposes or effect. When someone asks a *rhetorical question*, for instance, they are doing so only for effect, that is why they don't expect an answer.

To analyze something is to figuratively break it open and examine its parts in order to draw a *conclusion*. Let's look at an example of a job that you may have heard of. Someone who is a financial analyst looks at a company's current assets, the status of the current market, the company's past successes and failures, and then decides how the company can make more money. He or she *analyzes* the *financial* conditions of the situation to decide how the company can be successful; they break the situation open, examines the parts, and finally draw a conclusion.

A rhetorical analysis of an argument, then, is to examine the **rhetorical situation** surrounding a particular argument and draw a conclusion about its success. This assignment challenges students to examine the three parts of any given argument's rhetorical triangle (covered in Chapter 1, but listed below):

1. Author

2. Text

3. Audience

Students are also asked to examine the way the argument utilizes the three main rhetorical appeals:

1. Ethos

2. Logos

3. Pathos

And then, and only then, can the student accurately draw a conclusion about the argument's success. This kind of assignment challenges students to read arguments and consider whether or not they are actually successful; this assignment begs the question, is the argument convincing? Why or why not? And how exactly did you come to this conclusion?

Aristotle coined *ethos, logos,* and *pathos* as the three "artistic proofs" that a writer or speaker can use as means of persuading an audience.

Ethos: An Appeal to Authority

Ethos is the Greek word for "character." An author utilizes ethos when she attempts to convince the audience of her authority or credibility.

A good way to illustrate how the rhetorical appeals are at work in our everyday life is to look to advertisements. As previously stated, ads can be viewed as abbreviated arguments. How does the image below utilize ethos in order to sell the product?

Logos: An Appeal to Logic

The word "logic" is derived from the Greek word "logos," which is Greek for "word." An author utilizes logos when she attempts to convince the audience using logic or reason. An author might cite various studies, statistics, or experts in the field. How does the image below utilize logos in order to sell the product?

© *digitalreflections/Shutterstock.com*

Pathos: An Appeal to Emotion

The Greek word for "suffering" and "experience," an author utilizes the pathos appeal by attempting to convince the audience through appealing to their emotions. The words "pathetic" and "empathy" derive from the term pathos. The author might attempt to make the audience sympathetic, angry, fearful, or a variety of other emotions in order to convince them of the author's argument.

Buy an alarm system for your home today and protect your family from harm.

Reading Critically: Martin Luther King Jr.'s Letter from Birmingham Jail

One of the most persuasive and engaging speakers that ever lived was Martin Luther King, Jr. King's influence was so pervasive partly because he was consistently rhetorical in his language and communication. His word choice was always thoughtful. He kept his audience in mind and was a brilliant activist, leader, and speaker.

Partner Activity

Below you will find the first paragraph of a letter written by King while in-prisoned in Birmingham, Alabama. King brought the Civil Rights Movement to Birmingham, and eight clergymen from the area were up in arms about this. The clergymen published a statement about King's presence in their city, and King responded with the letter below.

April 16, 1963

My Dear Fellow Clergymen:

While confined here in the Birmingham city jail, I came across your recent statement calling my present activities "unwise and untimely." Seldom do I pause to answer criticism of my work and ideas. If I sought to answer all the criticisms that cross my desk, my secretaries would have little time for anything other than such correspondence in the course of the day, and I would have no time for constructive work. But since I feel that you are men of genuine good will and that your criticisms are sincerely set forth, I want to try to answer your statements in what I hope will be patient and reasonable terms.

Why is King's language in this letter so brilliant? Can you identify portions of the the excerpt that utilize the three rhetorical appeals? Which words stand out and why? Jot down some notes about what you and your partner noticed and tell the class what you came up with.

In noticing King's mastery of the language, remember to consider the three points of the rhetorical triangle as you revise your own work.

Activity

Imagine that you are enrolled in a math class where you have a B+ as your projected final grade. How would you convince your male, mid-thirties teacher to give you an A- for the final grade using all three of the rhetorical appeals? In the space that follows, write a few sentences that use the indicated appeal to convince the teacher. Remember to consider the rhetorical triangle—how does the author (you, in this case), the audience (your teacher), and the context (college math course with a mid-thirties male teacher) impact how to present your case?

Ethos Appeal:

_____

_____

_____

_____

Logos Appeal:

_____

_____

_____

_____

Pathos Appeal:

_____

_____

_____

_____

Advertisements: Abbreviated Visual Arguments

One type of rhetorical analysis is a *visual analysis*. Images, like the written word, can be crafted in a way that makes an argument. Advertisements, for instance, attempt to persuade the audience to purchase a product. This type of assignment is a great way to dip your toe into analysis. By using an image that we see every day and treating it like an argument worth analyzing, we can learn how to be critical of our world, particularly the media. Being critical is the first step in becoming a successful writer. Good critical thinking skills are vital in the early steps of the writing process.

Questions for Analyzing an Advertisement

The following questions will help you get started in your advertisement analysis project. They are adapted from Arthur Asa Berger's list in "Sex as Symbol in Fashion Advertising and Analyzing Signs and Sign Systems," Reading Culture 2nd edition. Diana George & John Trimbur, eds. NY: HarperCollins College Publishers, 1995: 163–164.

A.   What is the item being advertised, and what role does it play in American culture?

B.   What is the context of the ad–both where it was published (magazine, country) and when it was published?

C.   What is the general ambiance of the advertisement? What mood does it create? How does it do this?

D.   What is the design of the advertisement? Does it use axial balance or some other form? How are the basic components or elements of the advertisement arranged? (Axial balance refers to a design that symmetrically balances visual elements on either side of an invisible horizontal or vertical axis)

E.   What is the relationship that exists between pictorial elements and written material (the "copy"), and what does this relationship tell us?

F.   What is the spatiality in the advertisement? Is there a lot of "white space" or is the advertisement full of graphic and written elements (that is, "busy")?

G.   What signs and symbols do we find? What role do the various signs and symbols play in the advertisement?

H.   If there are figures (men, women, children, animals) in the advertisement, what are they like? What can be said about their facial expressions, poses, hairstyle, hair color, age, sex, ethnicity, education, occupation, relationships (of one to the other), and so on? What do these characteristics imply about the target audience?

I.   What does the background tell us? Where is the action in the advertisement taking place, and what significance does this background have?

J.   What action is taking place in the advertisement and what significance does this action have? (This might be described as the plot of the advertisement)

K.   What theme or themes do we find in the advertisement? What is the advertisement about? (The plot of an advertisement may involve a man and a woman drinking, but the theme might be jealousy, faithlessness, ambition, passion, etc.)

L.   What about the language used in the advertisement? Does it essentially provide information or generate some kind of emotional response? Or both? What techniques are used by the copywriter: for instance, humor, alliteration, "definitions" of life, comparisons, sexual innuendo?

M.   What typefaces (i.e. fonts) are used, and what impressions do these typefaces convey?

N.   What about aesthetic decisions? If the advertisement is a photograph, what kind of a shot is it? What significance do long shots, medium shots, close-ups have? What about the lighting, use of color, angle of the shot? What about the paper itself? Does it match the paper used in the rest of the magazine? Is it heavier? Does your ad span two pages or fold out?

O.   What sociological, political, economic, or cultural attitudes are indirectly reflected in the advertisement? An advertisement may be about a pair of blue jeans but it might, indirectly, reflect such matters as sexism, alienation, stereotyped thinking, conformism, generational conflict, loneliness, elitism, and so on.

Advertisement Analysis Peer Revision

Give your peer some notes and suggestions using the information below as a guide.

STEP ONE—Examining the Introduction: After reading the introduction, are you clear on the content and context of the advertisement?

The writer should clearly state the **genre** of the magazine as well as reveal the **audience** of the magazine. They should also explain how the genre and audience impact the analysis that they are about to present.

Perhaps even more importantly, the introduction should summarize and interpret the **content** of the ad—giving details on the product and how it is being advertised.

Lastly, the **thesis statement** should simultaneously reveal the analysis and assessment of the advertisement's rhetorical strategies.

STEP TWO—Examining the Body Paragraphs: Do the body paragraphs clearly and logically analyze the advertisement? Place an "S" next to sentences that summarize and an "A" next to paragraphs that analyze.

The essay's body should analyze the advertiser's intentions with the advertisement, that is to say, it should **analyze how well the advertiser achieved their goal** in persuading the reader to purchase it.

The body should not only **summarize and interpret** the claims and reasons implicit within the image, but it should **analyze and assess** how effective they are in selling the product.

STEP THREE—Examining the Conclusion: Does the conclusion merely repeat the essay's points, or does it include a pertinent, yet different example that proves the thesis?

The essay should end in a way that reinforces the essay's analysis and assessment but also brings in an additional example. Suggesting ways to improve the ad's effectiveness or even comparing the ad to a similar one are examples of this method.

Final Thoughts: Make sure that your peer's essay makes **a very specific claim** about the advertisement in the thesis and proves that claim in the rest of the essay using **evidence** from the advertisement itself. Give your partner some suggestions for how they can do this more effectively throughout the introduction, body, and conclusion.

Advertisement Analysis Rubric

	Analysis	Support	Summary	Context	Conventions	Organization
5	The student offers a clear, specific analysis on the ad's rhetorical strategies that is thoughtful and detailed. The analysis is comprehensive and examines a variety of strategies.	The student writes an accurate description of the ad to fully support their analysis. Support for their analysis is contextualized and integrated seamlessly.	The student offers a clear, informative summary of the ad's argument and reasons.	The student develops a context for his or her analysis with a description of the magazine and its readers, the date the magazine was published, and/or other relevant information. The contextual information is integrated into and used to support their analysis.	The student demonstrates exemplary control of language. The style is appropriate, sophisticated, and engaging. Errors are minimal, and the syntax is clear throughout the paper	The student incorporates a logical and fluid organizational plan. Sentences, paragraphs and transitions are cohesive and well-crafted within the introduction, body and conclusion.
4	The student usually offers a clear, specific analysis on the ad's rhetorical strategies that is usually thoughtful and detailed. The analysis may not be as comprehensive as it could be, but it is adequate.	The student uses a somewhat accurate description of the ad to support their analysis but some minor weaknesses may be present. Most are contextualized and integrated well.	The student offers an adequate summary of the ad's argument and reasons that is usually clear and informative.	The student develops a comprehensive context, but it may not always be integrated well. It is relevant to their analysis but not always directly supporting it.	The student demonstrates a consistent, above-average control of language. The style is appropriate, though not sophisticated. There are a few minor grammar and/or syntactical errors.	The student incorporates a logical and fluid organizational plan. Most sentences, paragraphs and transitions are cohesive and well-crafted within the introduction, body and conclusion.
3	The student offers an analysis on the ad's rhetorical strategies, but some portions may not be comprehensive, detailed and/or thoughtful.	The student uses an adequate description to support their analysis, but it is not usually contextualized or integrated well. A few portions of their analysis may be left unsupported.	The student offers an adequate summary of the ad's argument and reasons although it is occasionally not clear or informative.	The student provides an adequate amount of contextual information, but it is occasionally not integrated into or relevant to their analysis.	The student demonstrates a basic control of language. Style is mostly appropriate, though not engaging. Grammar and/or syntactical errors exist but do not interfere with the reader's comprehension.	The student maintains a logical organization. Some sentences and paragraphs are disjointed. Transitions are missing.
2	The student may summarize excessively instead of giving an analysis in many sections; some analysis may be present, but it is not adequate or overly vague.	The student frequently leaves their analysis unsupported. The small amount of description is not always accurate and are very often not contextualized or integrated adequately.	The student attempts to offer a summary of the ad's argument and reasons but is excessively vague or unclear.	The student provides a bit of contextual information but it is rarely integrated into or relevant to their analysis.	The student demonstrates a weak control of language and/or a style that is often inappropriate. Grammar and/or syntactical errors sometimes interfere with the reader's comprehension.	The student does not maintain a logically organized essay. Paragraphs are unfocused. Sentences and transitions are awkward.
1	The student summarizes excessively and/or no specific analysis is present.	The student rarely or never supports their analysis. If a description is present, it is not contextualized or integrated.	The student does not offer a clear summary of the ad's argument and reasons.	The student does not provide any context for their analysis.	The student demonstrates little to no control of language and/or little to no appropriate style. Grammar and/or syntactical errors consistently interfere with the reader's comprehension.	The student does not maintain a cohesive body of work. Paragraphs are often unfocused (incorporating multiple topics) and out of order. Sentences do not reflect syntactical awareness and transitions are missing.

Examining Sample Student Work: Advertisement Analysis Essay

Visual Analysis Essay

By Lauren Hives

People magazine is known across the United States for its numerous articles focusing on the personal lives of famous celebrities, celebrity lifestyle tips, and advertisements on perfumes, foods, and household items. Because *People* has a predominantly female demographic and women are usually the caregivers of a family, a number of the advertisements and articles cater to keeping families healthy as well as making their lives easier. An example of the depiction of these themes is found in a Campbell's Homestyle Chicken Noodle Soup advertisement published in the December 9, 2013 issue. In American culture, chicken noodle soup is used to help heal colds and to some, as comfort food. It is a very well known meal that is commonly depicted as a good meal to prepare to care for someone else. This advertisement not only achieves a goal of persuading its audience to purchase a healthy meal, but also relates itself to the closeness of family and how being together is an important part of the holiday season. The advertisement for Campbell's Homestyle Chicken Noodle Soup uses familiar imagery as well as colorful, descriptive texts to imply that their product is nutritious while associating it to the lifestyles of American families.

In the advertisement, it is clear the advertisers were attempting to create a cozy feeling for their audience by using colors that are relaxing to the eye and a recognizable backdrop. The colors tan, red, and brown are used heavily along with the natural colors of the vegetables to relate to the color scheme of the product itself, as well as to mute the background to make it less busy. These colors could easily be associated with the color scheme one finds in their homes making it relatable to the reader's own life. There is a lot of blank space throughout the page that some may find tranquil because advertisements with too many events taking place in the background could not only distract the reader from the main focus point and give the reader headaches. The background further suggests its affiliation with the average lifestyle by placing an image of the product on a kitchen table. It can be assumed that by using the interior of a kitchen as a background, the advertisers were trying to create a sense that a meal this quick and healthy can even be prepared in the comforts of your own home without any hassle to drop everything and pay for a meal at a restaurant. Parents in the United States are depicted as always concerned about having too little time to do the things needed to do to provide for their families' daily needs. To know a meal this easy could be prepared at no time at all could be very comforting.

The advertisers continue their portrayal of Campbell's Homestyle Chicken Noodle Soup being a hearty meal by the enlarged images they chose to use. One of the first images seen in the ad is a close-up of a giant bowl of the product placed in the middle of the page. The bowl is clean, white, and has a spoonful of the soup hovering over it. By using a clean, white, bowl and spoon, it is hinted that the soup can be prepared without enough effort to dirty the kitchen, something busy mothers would love to hear. In the image, the soup the ingredients can clearly be seen with fresh vegetables, noodles, spices, and strips of chicken that look well cooked and glossy in the soup's broth. Along with these images, there are images of onions, carrots, and celery on the outside of the bowl. With these images in mind, the vegetables further suggest the soup has nutritional value because of the healthy fresh vegetables. In American media, there are recurring images of a mother trying to make her children eat their vegetables, but to no avail. Now they can receive all kinds of vegetables by eating Campbell's soup. Coupled with the previously listed images, a message that all economic statuses of families can enjoy the soup is conveyed; the bowl does not appear to be a fancy or expensive or one that would be seen in a restaurant. Rather, it is a bowl could easily find at home in their kitchen cabinets.

The final tactics used to reach their targeted audiences are found within the language of the advertisement. This ad provides information about the nourishing benefits of Campbell's soup as well as generates an emotional response. The words "home-style" and "homemade" are used numerous times throughout the page, especially in the heading. Likewise, the heading is written in bold, capital letters, allowing the readers to see the heading if they did not notice the giant bowl of soup first. The heading "You Know You Love Homemade Chicken Noodle Soup, Especially When Someone Else Makes It" could relate to the ability of the soup to look tasty but taste exactly like the meals the caregiver of the house cooks from scratch. Equally important, the text underneath the heading reads, "brimming with farm grown vegetables and marinated roasted white meat chicken" uses logos to imply the soup is better for you than other soups because it is not made with processed ingredients. American foods are usually comprised of genetically modified vegetables and scientists have done multiple studies on whether these vegetables could be harmful to the body after long-term use. There is also controversy surrounding using white meat instead of dark meat.

Similar food related advertisements in *People* magazine feature happy families compromised of mothers, fathers, and their children that are seen eating a meal together around the family table. The only indicators of the products' nutritional values are seen in the captions and texts of the advertisement, yet the message of fitness and heartiness is conveyed. However, because of the lack of models and the careful detail on the ingredients of the product, the Campbell's Homestyle Chicken Noodle Soup advert could be more popular and reach a broader audience of not only parents but others who hold their well-being and relationships close to their hearts. Eating together is important but given the main focus of the advertisement is the soup, it is assumed the ingredients are even more important to their audiences. In addition to family models, other advertisers took it upon themselves to relate to the date when the publication was published by using statements such as "Good for the Christmas season" or even an ornament or two in the background. Nevertheless, with the lack of these decorations, the Campbell's advertisement can be seen throughout different times of the year and will still get its message across effectively.

Activity

Create a list of the above visual analysis essay's strengths and weaknesses. Use both the peer revision activity and rubric (previously) as a guide.

CHAPTER 5

You are a Better *Synthesizer* than You Realize

Now that you've mastered the skill of analysis, it's time to focus on *synthesis*. To *synthesize* is to combine various pieces to make a whole. In analytical writing, we use this term in contrast with analysis. If *analysis* is to break open a whole and examine the parts, then *synthesis* is to put the pieces of *analysis* together to draw some conclusion.

The Difference Between Synthesis and Argument

The practice of synthesis is very different from argument, which we will cover in the next chapter. But briefly, to argue is to take a stance and support that stance with evidence. To synthesize, one doesn't have to take or even have a particular stance on the subject, they only need to be able to objectively analyze the parts, then synthesize by drawing a conclusion.

For instance, here is a thesis that synthesizes:

> Although many college students find that using personal computers and laptops in the classroom is convenient for note taking, professors and administrators acknowledge that these devices often distract students from their coursework, leaving many to wonder whether the risk outweighs the reward.

And here is a thesis that argues on that same topic:

> Even though most professors and administrators are opposed to students using personal computers and tablets in the classroom because they may cause a distraction, tuition-paying students find them essential for note taking, research, and communicating with their professors; therefore, these devices should be accepted in college classrooms.

Analyzing and Synthesizing Controversial Issues

Students may often be confounded when a teacher asks them to analyze a controversial issue *without* taking a stance. This kind of activity can help to enhance your critical thinking skills, and most importantly, it allows students to put aside their own biases and research and write about a topic from the perspective of *discovery*. Instead of seeking sources that reinforce their own belief system, they seek sources that challenge it. This analytical process can be enlightening, to say the least.

One way that students can analyze an issue is to consider the **stakeholders**. A stakeholder is someone involved with this issue; this issue will impact their lives in some way; they have something *at stake*.

Stakeholder Example: Calorie Counts on Fast Food Menus

Consider the following research question: In light of the rising obesity rate in the US, should all fast food restaurants be required by law to put calorie counts on their menus?

The following groups can be considered *stakeholders* in this issue:

1. Customers
2. Fast food Corporate Executives
3. Fast food workers (managers and others)
4. Doctors

Each stakeholder will have their own set of circumstances and resulting perspective on the issue. One way to "unpack" an issue and begin your analysis and resulting synthesis is to carefully consider each perspective and properly define each stakeholder.

Below you will find one student's ideas on the perspectives on these stakeholders. The student makes some generalizations about these groups, but this is certainly a start to synthesizing this controversial issue.

Perspective of the Customers

The customers who frequent fast food restaurants are people who desire a quick, tasty, and inexpensive meal. With all of the information given to us from the media on how unhealthy fast food tends to be, these customers probably understand this commonly accepted fact. They are probably not going to these restaurants seeking a healthy meal. With that being said, today's consumers value information. The more information, the better. With the internet encompassing our daily lives, customers are used to instant information, and they have come to expect it. When it comes to including calorie counts on the menu, the customers will probably be apathetic. Although they desire information quickly, they usually do not go to fast food restaurants thinking about calorie counts or fat grams. Although a small portion customers will want to be more health-conscious, they can seek the calorie counts online. Ultimately, most fast food customers may not agree that we need a law requiring calorie counts be put on fast food menus.

Perspective of the Fast Food Corporate Executives

The fast food corporate executives are ultimately concerned with the bottom line. Including calorie counts on menus will cost a lot of money: the calories have to be counted up by dietitians who will require a fee; menus have to be reprinted and manufactured, which will also cost money; some customers may even stop dining at the restaurants once they are confronted with the high calorie counts. Fast food executives will probably not support a law requiring calorie counts on menus. They would not want any regulations at all on the way they choose to do business. The executives may claim that the best strategy is to consider the free market's potential impact instead of creating a new regulation. Over time, customers may come to expect calories on menus, which would ultimately force executives to make changes.

Perspective of the Fast Food Workers

Fast food workers, including managers and other employees, are most concerned with keeping their jobs. If customers are not happy and stop dining at the restaurant, then profits go down, and employees may lose their jobs. On the other hand, if profits go up, employees may get raises. Fast food workers probably would support a law that requires calorie counts on menus. If some customers are apathetic about calorie counts on menus, and other customers are happy to have more information, then it's safe to assume that profits will either stay the same or go up from these changes. A large drop in profits is not likely, so the workers' jobs will probably be even more secure if these changes are made.

Perspective of Doctors

One could argue that each of these groups is most concerned with money, and you could make that case for doctors, perhaps. However, doctors take an oath to "do no harm." It is safe to assume that doctors want the best for their patients. They want their patients to be healthy, and they are probably very concerned about the obesity crisis in particular, probably more than any other stakeholder in this controversy. Since their first priority is health, doctors would undoubtedly support this the law to require calorie counts on fast food menus. Doctors may claim that informing customers of how unhealthy the food is would prevent them from eating it; thus, improving patients' health.

Questions for Discussion

1. Who are the stakeholders involved in the controversy over sexism in beauty pageants?

2. Consider the following research questions to guide you: Are beauty pageants appropriate in modern day society, considering that many view them as a sexist, misogynistic activity that objectifies women? What would the various stakeholders have to say about this issue?

Essay Mapping with This American Life's Podcast, "Use Only as Directed"

This activity asks you to think about this podcast *rhetorically*, that is, to examine the words and strategies used to make this piece effective in its purpose, which is to analyze and eventually synthesize the controversial use of a popular pain relief medicine.

Use the QR code to access the podcast with your smartphone. You can choose the option to listen to the podcast or read a transcript.

Prologue:

1. The prologue does a nice job of defining the controversy, which is something that students should do in their analytical essays. How do the speakers define the controversy in the prologue? What IS the controversy and HOW do they reveal it?

2. Based on what you have heard so far in the podcast's prologue, what would you say is the purpose? To inform? Argue? Analyze? How do you know?

3. What strategy is being used to introduce the controversy? What grabs your attention in the introduction? Is it effective? Why or why not?

4. Create a one sentence "thesis statement" based on what you have heard so far.

5. Even though the prologue isn't taking a position on the controversy, it does make several analytical claims, which is something that students should do in their analytical essay. What are the two central claims?

6. Based on what you've heard so far, what *is* a potential argument for this topic? What would the next hypothetical podcast potentially argue?

Act One:

1. How do the speakers reveal that the stakes are high with this issue? What comparison do they make and is it effective in raising the stakes?

2. The speakers make a generalization about all medicines and patients to illustrate their point. Describe how this method is effective in illustrating how dangerous acetaminophen is.

3. The speakers give a history of this controversy. What does that history reveal? And how is it supporting their thesis or central claim?

4. The speakers do a nice job of anticipating what the listeners may be thinking or wondering. In one case, they bring up the question suicide: how can the researchers be certain that all of these deaths aren't due to suicide? They refute that idea thoroughly. What strategies do they use to refute it? Do they refute it respectfully and convincingly?

5. Towards the end of Act One, the speakers appear to assign blame. Who may be to blame and how do the speakers manage to do this without appearing to make an argument on the controversy?

Act Two:

1. In this Act, the speakers raise the stakes even further. How do they do this? And what kind of rhetorical appeals are being utilized here? Give specific examples. Are they effective in synthesizing (not arguing on) this issue)?

2. The speakers detail McNeil's efforts in making dosing more clear on the package of Tylenol. Does this make you sympathetic to the company? Why or why not? Was this a good strategy for Act Two in particular?

3. The podcast ends with a description of the "proliferation of products." What do the speakers mean by this? And why was this strategy so effective in the conclusion of the podcast?

Issue Analysis Peer Revision

No matter what the assignment is, revising a friend's essay can be helpful in developing your own writing skills. Not to mention that getting feedback on your work can help out tremendously. The common research paper that analyzes controversial issues is a useful assignment to sharpen your critical thinking skills and synthesize your research and ideas. The activity below will help you to give your partner some useful feedback on that kind of assignment. Answer the following questions on a separate sheet to give your partner, and don't be afraid to write directly on their draft as well!

STEP ONE—Evaluating for Content: As you read your partner's draft, think about the following questions that reference CONTENT.

STEP TWO—Examining the Introduction Paragraph

Does the paragraph make the controversy clear? Meaning, does it explain WHAT is up for DEBATE and clearly show why this issue is worth pursuing? How so?

Does it provide an adequate CONTEXT? Or perhaps some background information? Is that working well? Why?

Does it accurately describe WHO the stakeholders are and WHAT is at stake, exactly?

STEP THREE—Examining the Thesis Statement:

Does synthesize the various sub-issues or perspectives covered in the essay from what you can tell? Why or why not?

Is it clear, specific, and focused? Why or why not? How could they improve the thesis?

Does it make clear that this issue is not merely "two sided" but has multiple parts or include multiple stakeholders?

After reading the essay, give them some suggestions on how to make their thesis more "analytical."

STEP FOUR—Examining the Body Paragraphs:

Are they cohesive and focused? Meaning, do they clearly analyze each sub-issue without "jumping around" to other sub-issues? Why or why not? How do you recommend that they focus their points more accurately?

Is a well-developed, careful analysis of each "part" or "stakeholder" present? Or, does it seem like something is missing? What else should they include to make the analysis more developed?

Are their claims supported with relevant and accurate evidence in the form of summary, paraphrases and quotes? Are those pieces of evidence actually SUPPORTING or PROVING their claims? How could they potentially improve?

Are the quotes and statistics well-integrated? Give examples of how they could potentially improve.

Most importantly, does the essay draw unique conclusions based on the source material provided? Or, does the essay seem more like a string of source summaries? How could they improve?

STEP FIVE—Examining the Conclusion Paragraph

Does the conclusion paragraph include an accurate yet brief summary of the essay's main points? If the summary is excessive, then what should they potentially eliminate?

Does it look the future with this controversy and show how this controversy relates to larger issues in society? How could they potentially improve?

Does it leave you with something to think about? Whether it's the limitations of this issue or the implications of the controversy if nothing is done?

Sample Student Work: Issue Analysis Essay

What is wrong with raising my child as a vegetarian?

By Consuelo Gallardo

"Death by Veganism" reads a New York Times headline from 2007 written by the advocate of

traditional food Nina Planck, reporting the tragic decease of Crown Shakur, a six-weeks-old boy from

Atlanta who starved to death when his strict-vegan parents fed him solely with soy-milk and apple juice.

Unfortunately for this kid, those who were supposed to provide him the best conditions to grow up

healthy lacked of qualified information and guidance to administrate a delicate diet like this one; and

if this was not enough, there have been several cases throughout the world where innocent infants are

forced to pay for the poor judgement of those who prefer developing an ethical relationship with non-

human animals instead of offering their own babies the most complete and beneficial variety of essential

nutrients.

According to the Oxford dictionary, a vegetarian is "A person who does not eat meat or fish, and sometimes other animal products, especially for moral, religious, or health reasons." As time passes by there are more and more people following this kind of diet, substituting animal products for plant products, claiming that it is a healthier way to live since it helps lowering the rate of certain diseases like obesity, diabetes, colon cancer, among others.

Even if this "movement" bases itself on scientific research ensuring that a vegetarian diet provides all essential nutrients, on the other hand it is possible to find scientific sources as well that demonstrate how this kind of diet, if not correctly planned, can be actually harmful at some ages, like childhood and adolescence, considering the fact that bodies are still growing. While most experts agree that in some cases vegetarianism might be appropriate for children, those vegetarian parents that choose this lifestyle for their kids without enough education to do so tend to detriment these diets basically by not heeding children's delicate nutritional needs.

First of all, for the purpose of this essay it is important to state the difference between two major terms- vegetarianism and veganism. As it was stated above, vegetarians are those who do not eat meat, although it is possible for them to consume dairy products and eggs, giving them the chance to include some variety into their diets. Conversely, there is a different group that do not only restrict themselves from eating meat but they also reject any animal product. This specific group will be denoted as vegans, and their feeding consists entirely on plant-based foodstuff.

Within the complex discussion of whether a vegetarian or vegan diet is appropriate for kids, those who consider it inappropriate base their arguments on the risks that this choice may convey, which are mostly hazardous for bodies in development. It is important to note that most of these risks appear whenever there is a nutritional imbalance and diets are not meeting their objectives. An example of this is an article published in the New York Times in 2012 written by Nina Planck, "A choice with definite risks". Planck argues that in life there are some things that cannot be replaced, and for her real food is one. This idea in particular does not add credibility to her argument because when analyzing her qualification to write about this issue one can discover that she is a farmer's daughter and the owner of an international farmer's market, so of course Planck encourages people to feed their children with traditional food.

Even if Nina Planck acknowledges that vegetarianism might be a wise choice for adults, she also criticizes strongly those parents that "drag" their children within this moral. Utilizing some medical information, the author of this article discusses how the lack of crucial nutrients may affect in short and long-term infant's health, especially if they or their mothers are vegans. For example, she mentions that "the breast milk of vegan mothers is dramatically lower in a critical brain fat, DHA, than the milk of an omnivorous mother." Also, she says that "the quantity and bio-availability of other nutrients, such as calcium and protein, are superior when consumed from animal rather than plant sources." And this is where she recognizes that while it is possible to survive on a diet "including high-quality dairy and eggs", one based on plants alone is appropriate only for herbivores. So, in synthesis, one can see that most of the opposition's arguments are based on the idea that plant-based diets are unable to provide all the essential nutrients, and this is why it is important to at least include some eggs or dairy products to avoid the dreaded lack of nutrients.

Now, knowing this, why is there a controversy anyway if specialists state that most vegetarian diets may be appropriate? Part of the answer has to do with the key word balance. According to the American Dietetic Association and Dietitians of Canada, "a carefully planned vegetarian diet can be healthy and suitable from the nutritional point of view and can have benefits in the prevention and treatment of certain diseases." This statement is also backed up by evidence provided on Anna Sherratt's article "Vegetarians and their children". Here, Sherratt cites famous studies throughout the world published in peer-reviewed scientific journals that "put to rest the idea of the vegetarian child as starved and underdeveloped." First she mentions Thane and Bates, who concluded that 'Given a balanced diet, adequate nutritional intakes and status can be maintained without eating meat'. Second, Leung *et al.* claimed that 'an absence of growth retardation and a low prevalence of nutrient deficiency suggest that a Chinese vegetarian diet can be suitable for fast-growing children'. Then, Hebbelinck *et al.* wrote 'In conclusion, the results of this study support the view that a lactoovovegetarian diet (including fruits, vegetables, fish, seeds, nuts, eggs and dairy) sustains adequate physical grow and maturation'. Finally, Sanders and Reddy suggested that 'there is no doubt that a properly selected vegetarian diet can meet all the requirements of growing children'. One can see that each of these studies concluded that vegetarian diets might be appropriate as long as they are selected and planned, so once again the problem is not whether your child is vegetarian or not but whether you as a parent are responsible or not.

The ADA also indicated that "in some cases, the use of fortified foods or supplements may be useful in covering the recommendations for each nutrient." This last sentence makes noise for some omnivores who argue that the consumption of supplements should not be taken lightly; and to fulfill its real purpose, this is to add nutrients to a diet, they must be managed with great delicacy. Supplements, according to the FDA, need to be acquired from physicians to ensure a correct administration, because there might be harmful consequences when people take high or low doses of supplemental nutrients such as Vitamin A, Vitamin D and iron. So again, according to experts a responsible and educated guidance makes the difference between healthy and malnourished children.

What is the problem then with those parents that – even if they could have information at hand – fail administering vegetarian diets to their babies? Let us revisit the initial case of Crown Shakur. It was said that, unfortunately, there have been several occasions like this one where children die malnourished mainly due to vegetarian or vegan diets that they were following. Louise, an eleven-month-old baby girl died in 2008 due to vitamin deficiency after being fed only on breastmilk. Her parents, strict

vegetarians, had adopted this lifestyle after a TV show about cows being slaughtered, which reflects an

obvious absence of necessary education. They were formalized and sent to jail. Areni, a nine-month-

old baby girl suffered a similar situation in 2000 when her vegetarian parents thought she only needed

"sun and fruits", and consequently caused her death. Nicolas Dos Santos, a BDA pediatric dietician

stated that this fruit-based diet "is not a diet a child should be put on." Finally, Caleb, a six-month-old

baby boy died in 2002 due to vitamin B_{12} deficiency when his strict vegan mother whose diet was free

of meat, fish, and dairy products was breastfeeding him. All of these are clear examples of how lack of

education can trigger regrettable events, because clearly these parents did not have the correct advice to

feed their kids on a healthy and stable vegetarian or vegan diet.

When saying that a "vegetarian diet" is dangerous for children, there is not enough specificity,

because nowadays there are at least four different types of vegetarian diets determined by animal

products they do or do not consume. In other words, the negative perception of vegetarianism as a

threat for infants has to do practically with the misuse of the term. That is the main reason why in

this essay the first thing was to differentiate between vegetarians and vegans, because now it is possible

to suggest that vegetarian diets are more capable of providing essential nutrients and thus, avoid

malnourishing, rickets, brain damage, and all those consequences found on terribly-planned vegan

diets. They key, again, is balance. Crown Shakur and all the babies that passed away due to veganism

could now be alive if their parents would have been conscious and aware that in order to eliminate the

consumption of meat, it is crucial to substitute it and it's nutrients with other animal products; and also,

in some cases, with supplements, but all of these with extreme care and guidance. It is not an issue of an

evil intention from the parents, it is not that they are crazy, or that they prefer their children to die than

to put some animals in pain, it is just that there is not enough spread of the imperative information to provide a vegetarian diet to a kid. According to experts, these diets might be appropriate, but not for everybody, because they require a detailed study before and while it is followed. So, in future situations, instead of just criticizing and punishing vegetarian parents with vegetarian children, let us also provide more education for them and for everybody; in that way kids like Crown, Louise, Areni, Caleb, and others that remain anonymous will have the chance to live and to become healthy, strong, and normal adults.

Works Cited

Anton-Paduraru, Dana-Teodora, et al. "Vegetarian Diet in Children." *Romanian Journal of Pediatrics* 63.4 (2014): 357–361. *Academic Search Complete*. Web. 27 Sept. 2015.

Farley, Dixie. *Vegetarian diets: the pluses and the pitfalls*. Rockville: Dpt. of Health and Human Services, Public Health Service, Food and Drug Administration, 1994. Print.

Planck, Nina. "A Choice With Definite Risks." *New York Times*. The New York Times Company, 17 Ap. 2012. Web. 27 Sep. 2015.

Planck, Nina. "Death By Veganism." *New York Times*. The New York Times Company, 21 May 2007. Web. 15 Nov. 2015

Queen, Patricia, and Carol Lang. *Handbook of pediatric nutrition*. Gaithersburg, MD: Aspen Publishers, 1993. Print.

Sherratt, Anna. "Vegetarians and Their Children." *Journal of Applied Philosophy* 24.4 (2007): 425–434. Academic Search Complete. Web. 15 Nov. 2015.

Activity

Create a list of the above essay's strengths and weaknesses. Use the peer revision activity above as a guide.

Questions for Discussion

Reflect on the peer revision process:

1. What do you find most useful about the peer revision process? The sample essay examination?

2. How can we be the best peer revisers possible? What are some best practices in your opinion?

3. Describe your own personal revision process. What works and what doesn't?

4. What are some of your strengths that you have discovered through the revision process?

5. What are some of your weaknesses that you have discovered through the revision process?

Argument Analysis: Where Do I Start?

When your teacher asks you to write a rhetorical analysis (also called an argument analysis) essay, it is meant to test your knowledge of argumentation effectiveness, logical fallacy use, and identification of the rhetorical appeals.

These kinds of critical thinking skills are vital to your success, not only in your composition class, but in all college courses and in all of your professional activities outside of college. Every single job that I can think of involves communication of some kind. This assignment allows you to consider language and communication as rhetorical devices that impact the way your audience views you, whether that's requesting copies from the office secretary or explaining to your boss why you deserve an higher salary.

In an earlier chapter, you read Anne Lamot's essay called *Shitty First Drafts*. Now is a great time to try out that strategy!

Answering the questions below will help you to get started. On a separate page, answer the questions in paragraph format. When you're done, you will have your first draft complete!

Remember: you are NOT explaining why the argument is *wrong* or *right,* but explaining how and why the argumentation style is successful or unsuccessful in convincing the audience.

1. The first thing to do is read and study the article you have chosen. Based on your reading, ***you must pinpoint the argument in the text***; in other words, you have to decide what you think the author is trying to persuade the audience to think or do. In the space below, describe what you believe to be the author's purpose. What is their central claim? What are their reasons to support that claim? Summarize the author's "point."

2. The second step is to ***identify the author's claims and evidence***. Write the letter "C" next to all sections in the article that are claims and the letter "E" next to all sections that serve as evidence to support those claims. Look at the ***ratio of evidence to claims***. Are there any claims that lack evidence? Quote them and explain how the author could have improved.

3. Then, take a closer look at the author's evidence and answer the following questions: What type of evidence is the author using? Statistics? Personal stories? Etc. What type of **rhetorical appeal** is the author using: logos, ethos, or pathos? Is it working? Is it convincing? Why or why not? Pick out several sections from the article, quote them here, and then give your analysis.

Rhetorical Analysis Peer Revision

Getting someone else to read your work is an often overlooked but very useful step in the writing process. We may think that our writing is perfectly clear and logical, but when classmate reads it, you can become enlightened about your work.

For a rhetorical analysis essay, follow these three steps to help your partner out. Write plenty of constructive comments directly on their essay, and don't be shy about your critique! You are both students, and no one expects your work to be perfect.

STEP ONE—Examining the Analysis: Read your partner's essay and focus mainly on their analysis.

Is the analysis adequate? Or mostly summary?

Does it discuss a variety of rhetorical strategies, errors in logic, language issues, etc?

Is it clear and easy to understand? Clarity is important, but you'll want to focus mainly on ***content.***

STEP TWO—Considering the Essay Requirements: Is your partner's draft fulfilling the ***requirements*** detailed on the assignment sheet provided? Read the assignment sheet section by section and give them some notes on what they might be missing.

STEP THREE—Thinking about Quality: Think about the ***quality*** of the essay as a whole. Circle the portions of the rubric that you think apply to your partner's draft. You can circle an entire "box" or a few different sentences from each "box"—whatever best describes their draft.

Rhetorical Analysis Rubric

Analyzing written arguments is great practice for accurate and successful communication, and using a rubric for writing this essay can prevent you from feeling anxious or wondering if you "did it right." Use the rubric below to assess the quality of a rhetorical analysis, whether it is your own, a sample, or one of your peers' essays.

	Analysis	Support	Summary	Context	Conventions	Organization
5	The student offers a clear, specific analysis on the author's rhetorical strategies that is thoughtful and detailed. The analysis is comprehensive and examines a variety of strategies.	The student uses accurate paraphrases and quotations to fully support their analysis. They are contextualized and integrated seamlessly.	The student offers a clear, informative summary of the author's central claims and reasons.	The student develops a context for his or her analysis through a description of the author's qualifications, the potential biases of the publication, the date the article was written, and/or other relevant information. The contextual information is integrated into and used to support their analysis.	The student demonstrates exemplary control of language. The style is appropriate, sophisticated, and engaging. Errors are minimal, and the syntax is clear throughout the paper	The student incorporates a logical and fluid organizational plan. Sentences, paragraphs and transitions are cohesive and well-crafted within the introduction, body and conclusion.
4	The student usually offers a clear, specific analysis on the author's rhetorical strategies that is usually thoughtful and detailed. The analysis may not be as comprehensive as it could be, but it is adequate.	The student uses somewhat accurate paraphrases and quotations to support their analysis but some minor weaknesses may be present. Most are contextualized and integrated well.	The student offers an adequate summary of the author's central claims and reasons that is usually clear and informative.	The student develops a comprehensive context, but it may not always be integrated well. It is relevant to their analysis but not always directly supporting it.	The student demonstrates a consistent, above-average control of language. The style is appropriate, though not sophisticated. There are a few minor grammar and/or syntactical errors.	The student incorporates a logical and fluid organizational plan. Most sentences, paragraphs and transitions are cohesive and well-crafted within the introduction, body and conclusion.
3	The student offers an analysis on the author's rhetorical strategies, but some portions may not be comprehensive, detailed and/or thoughtful.	The student uses adequate quotes and paraphrases to support their analysis, but some are not contextualized or integrated well. A few portions of their analysis may be left unsupported.	The student offers an adequate summary of the author's central claims and reasons although it is occasionally vague or informative.	The student provides an adequate amount of contextual information, but it is occasionally not integrated into or relevant to their analysis.	The student demonstrates a basic control of language. Style is mostly appropriate, though not engaging. Grammar and/or syntactical errors exist but do not interfere with the reader's comprehension.	The student maintains a logical organization. Some sentences and paragraphs are disjointed. Transitions are missing.
2	The student may summarize excessively instead of giving an analysis in many sections; some analysis may be present, but it is not adequate or overly vague.	The student frequently leaves their analysis unsupported. The few quotes and paraphrases present are not always accurate and are very often not contextualized or integrated adequately.	The student attempts to offer a summary of the author's central claims and reasons but is excessively vague or unclear.	The student provides a bit of contextual information but it is rarely integrated into or relevant to their analysis.	The student demonstrates a weak control of language and/or a style that is often inappropriate. Grammar and/or syntactical errors sometimes interfere with the reader's comprehension.	The student does not maintain a logically organized essay. Paragraphs are unfocused. Sentences and transitions are awkward.
1	The student summarizes excessively and/or no specific analysis is present.	The student rarely or never supports their analysis. If quotes or paraphrases are present, they are not contextualized or integrated.	The student does not offer a clear summary of the author's claims and reasons.	The student does not provide any context for their analysis.	The student demonstrates little to no control of language and/or little to no appropriate style. Grammar and/or syntactical errors consistently interfere with the reader's comprehension.	The student does not maintain a cohesive body of work. Paragraphs are often unfocused (incorporating multiple topics) and out of order. Sentences do not reflect syntactical awareness and transitions are missing.

Sample Student Work: Rhetorical Analysis Essay

Rhetorical Analysis of "Time to Question Sanity of Death Penalty"

By Shelby St. Germain

The article, "Time to Question Sanity of Death Penalty", was published on July 26, 2015 to "Death Row Stories", a column featured on CNN. Phillip Holloway, a legal analyst for CNN, wrote the article expressing his views on the effectiveness of the death penalty. Before becoming an analyst for CNN, Phillip Holloway upheld many different occupations. After graduating from law school, Holloway went on to serve as an officer and judge advocate in the U.S. Navy. He then became a police officer, and later a prosecutor, opening his own law firm in Georgia. Throughout all of these occupations, Holloway obtained a wide range of experience in legal matters which qualifies him to make an assertion on the effectiveness of the death penalty. The recent 2012 Chicago movie theater shooting sparked his argument stating that there are cheaper, more justifying, precautionary, and practical ways to punish a capital offender than sentencing the death penalty. Phillip Holloway's article, "Time to Question Sanity of Death Penalty", is incredibly effective in arguing that the death penalty is not the most practical punishment for capital offenders through his use of pathos, personal stories and testimonies, and accredited and factual statistics.

Holloway states, "I've never been to prison, but having dealt regularly with prisoners, it is clear that prison life is hard—very hard…" In his opening argument, Holloway lets his audience know that he is honest. By stating that he has not been to prison, he establishes that although his opinions are not from personal experience, he does have authority on the subject because of his extensive experience in legal matters. Immediately, Holloway has gained the trust of his audience by being honest, yet factual.

Holloway explains that he has no problem with criminals being punished. He simply believes the death penalty is not as penalizing of a punishment as life without parole. He supports this claim with evidence from a death row inmate in Missouri who was recently executed. The inmate stated hours before his execution "for those who remain on death row, understand that everyone is going to die… Statistically speaking, we have a much easier death than most, so I encourage you to embrace it and celebrate our true liberation before society figures it out and condemns us to life without parole, and we too will die a lingering death." The use of this death row inmates' testimony serves as a great tool to aid in his argument. The inmate agrees with Holloway's claim stating that he, a prisoner, realized death row is not as punitive as life without parole precisely proving Holloway's point.

Holloway also argues that the death penalty is much more expensive, "costing taxpayers far more than prosecutions seeking life without parole." This appeals to his audience's sense of emotions because it affects them personally. Although we do not want to, everyone in the United States must pay taxes and some may see this use of tax dollars as a waste. By explaining that the death penalty is more expensive, Holloway is gaining support of his tax paying audience. He also makes a good use of his argument by offering the monetary difference between the death penalty prosecutor's cost and the life without parole prosecutors' cost.

Holloway introduces the statistic that "…The state will shell out approximately $3.5 million, as opposed to an average of $150,000 if the state had not sought the death penalty," Holloway quotes the American Civil Liberties Union, furthering his credibility of his claim. He goes on to prove his argument by explaining that the amount of time spent in the courtroom for prosecuting a death penalty case versus a life without parole case if far more time consuming. This evidence alone would allow for a valid argument because it appeals to the readers' sense of pathos…

Holloway also states that the longer the trial, the longer the jurors must attend, the longer the courtroom is tied up, and the longer the staff must be of use. At some point in time, most people will be responsible for jury duty, which causes complications in the average persons' life. This is an excellent way for Holloway to appeal to anyone who has been responsible, and for anyone who will one day be responsible for jury duty. Holloway strategically constructs his argument to appeal to the reader's sense of emotions while also providing evidence for all of his claims.

Although many are firm believers in the death penalty, it is not always taken into account that the death penalty affects more than the individual on death row. Holloway explains that most death penalty cases take, on average, twenty-five years to reach a resolution. This drawn out process can be horrific to the victims, and families of victims waiting to receive justice for the criminals' actions. This is an excellent way to appeal to the readers' emotions. It allows the reader to feel sympathy for the families and the victims and strengthens Holloway's argument because if there was no death penalty, this would not be an issue.

He explains, "In fact, in Colorado, the trial portion of the process alone is six times longer than if the state were seeking life without parole." Although his audience is not restricted to people in Colorado, he is gaining a mass of followers by relating it to both the incident in Colorado, and families of murdered victims. Again, Holloway makes excellent use of pathos by directly relating how the death penalty affects many individuals other than the criminal. It is apparent that Holloway is an exceptional writer by the way he cohesively and articulately structures and organizes his claims to appeal to his audiences' emotions.

Holloway argues another valid point; the death penalty is not evenly applied throughout the United States. He proves this claim by giving evidence that "only 31 of the 50 United States employ capital punishment." This is another valid point in Holloway's article. It allows the reader to question why we have such a law if it is not applied to everyone in the United States, creating agreement with Holloway's point. Giving such specific evidence about the laws dealing with capital punishment, Holloway not only gains trust from his readers, but he portrays that he is well educated and up to date on the laws dealing with the death penalty.

He goes on to explain that, "even in some of the states that allow capital punishment, prosecutors can decide against pursing a death sentence." This clearly proves his claim that the death penalty is not evenly applied in all states, or at all in fact. Holloway gives an example of a case tried in Cobb County, Georgia where a child was left in a hot car to die. This would be a good example, but Holloway fails to explain the case. He merely assumes that the audience is familiar with the case and proceeds to explain that the death penalty cannot be used in Georgia. This appears to be Holloway's first mistake. He does not introduce the case he uses as an example, which can be confusing to his audience. The reader does not know the full story behind the incident, which can leave questions unanswered. Although he uses evidence to prove his claim, Holloway does not fully inform the reader of the situation, which could be considered fatal to his argument.

Holloway also argues that the death penalty can be detrimental to some individuals. Although many precautions and detective work is done, mistakes do happen, and sometimes, innocent people end up on death row. Holloway supports this claim with statistical evidence. "There have been 154 verified cases of death row exonerations since 1973." This proves Holloways claim to the fullest extent. He uses factual information to appeal to his reader's sense of emotion. Although precautions were taken, somewhere during the process, something was missed, and an innocent individual lost his life. This appeals to the reader's sense of ethos in more ways than one. The families who experienced this first hand would be the first ones to agree that the death penalty should be outlawed. Also, any sympathetic individual would find this heartbreaking; that a life was lost for no reason. This leaves reason for anyone who advocates the death penalty to reconsider his or her thought process.

Holloway introduces more statistics proving this claim. He states that, "a study last year found that, at a conservative estimate, more than 4% of inmates sentenced to death in the United States are probably innocent." This four percent is separate from the 154 cases that have been verified. While this 4% may not seem like a lot, the years that these innocent men and women lost can never be replaced. These statistics are vital to Mr. Holloways claims. They prove that innocent individuals have served unnecessary time, and it some more unfortunate cases; they have lost their lives. Again, this appeals to the reader's sense of pathos. No one wants to see someone put away, or put to death, for something that they did not do, but more importantly... the families of these men and women lost time that they will never get back. Holloway, yet again, has done an excellent job of getting the reader on his side of the argument by the use of pathos. Although the death penalty may be favorable to some, this evidence must be acknowledged because it is factual and certainly disheartening.

In closing, Holloway states, "While the death penalty is neither 'cruel,' when taking into account the cruelty so often inflicted on the victim, nor 'unusual,' in that it has been around for millennia, there are simply too many practical reasons for states to curtail or abandon their use of the death penalty." Although he does a good job of closing his argument, it is merely an opinion. He believes that the death penalty is not cruel or unusual. Although some may agree with his viewpoint, this is a weak point in his article because it is not backed up with evidence. He claims that the criminal justice system and the families of the victims would be the biggest beneficiaries, but here again, it is merely his opinion, which is a weak point in this article.

Perhaps the most powerful and clutching statement in Holloway's article is the very last. He states, after his claim that even individuals who are facing murder charges do not necessarily fear the death penalty, "Just ask Chattanooga or Charleston." Holloway explains that Jamie Hood, recently convicted of the murder of a cop, defended himself and won. Hood happily accepted the life without parole sentence he plead for. Holloway stated that, "this further illustrates that capital punishment does not deter individuals who are intent on murder." By providing this example to his audience he furthers his argument of the death penalty being ineffective. It does not instill the fear that it should; not even for murders, so why have it? Again, everyone is entitled to their own opinion, but Holloway proves his point very effectively.

A well written, open-minded article takes time and effort to construct. In my opinion, Holloway does an excellent job of this. He is respectful in his delivery and supports his claims with valid and useful evidence. Although Mr. Holloway may not have the agreement of his audience through every point he makes, he certainly puts up a good fight in trying to obtain their agreement. He makes excellent use of the reader's sense of pathos, and stays firm in his beliefs. I believe that except for a couple unsupported opinions, Holloway has done an excellent job of arguing why the death penalty is not the most effective and reliable form of punishment.

Works Cited

Holloway, Phillip. "Time to Question Sanity of Death Penalty." CNN.com. CNN, 26 July 2015. Web.

19 Oct. 2015.

Activity

Make a list of the essay's strengths and weaknesses. Use both the peer revision activity and rubric (above) as a guide.

Questions for Discussion

Reflect on your progress as a writer and analytical thinker.

1.   Did the "where the heck do I start" activity help you get started?

2.   What was the most difficult part of analyzing an argument?

3.   How could you overcome those difficulties in the future?

4.   What was the easiest part of analyzing an argument?

5.   How can you continue to develop those strengths?

6.   How did analyzing an argument prepare you to write your own?

CHAPTER 6

You are a Better *Arguer* than You Realize

As an academic writer, writing your own argument will represent a culmination of your analytical and critical thinking skill building. This chapter will hopefully allow you to see that writing an argument, although it can seem overwhelming, can be easier than you might think. There are several simple strategies presented in this chapter that can allow students to see that they are better arguers than they realize.

Introduction to Argumentation: Writing Your Own Argument

Aristotle's *Rhetoric* was and still is a profoundly influential work that helps us to use language effectively in both oral and written communication. Aristotle was particularly interested in using language as a means to persuade. Aristotle teaches us about the "rhetorical situation" in order to best understand how we can persuade a given audience of something at a particular time in space. See Chapter 1 for more information on the "rhetorical situation."

Rhetoricians like Aristotle aren't necessarily interested in being persuasive through manipulation, but he and other rhetoric scholars acknowledge the need for a particular kind of language in order to convey the truth. One of the most accurate definitions of "argument" is found in the textbook *Writing Arguments:*

Argument combines truth-seeking with persuasion.

Misconceptions about Argument

"Argument" is a term that is difficult to define. Merriam-Webster's attempts to do so with these varying definitions:

> A statement or series of statements for or against something.
> A discussion in which people express different opinions about something.
> An angry disagreement.

The problem with these definitions is that they represent common misconceptions about intelligent argumentation, which is neither a series of statements, a discussion, nor an angry disagreement. "Statements" and "discussion" are a bit too vague to describe argumentation properly, and "anger" is never a part of intelligent argument. Claiming that argument is to discuss why one is "for" or "against" something is far too simplistic and leaves no room for circumstance or context. Finally, expressing opinion is far from argumentation; that sounds more like a conversation than an argument.

Misconception #1: To Argue is to Describe the Pros and Cons

The phrase "pros and cons" is Latin for the phrase *pro et contra*, which roughly means "for and against." Any person could describe why someone might be for or against a certain issue. Controversies are rarely obvious. If they were obvious, they wouldn't be controversial. To argue a particular stance is much more complex. You wouldn't just *describe* the pros and cons, but would instead *support your stance, acknowledge the opposition* (including the valid points), and then *refute* it.

Misconception #2: To Argue is to Give One's Opinion

To give an opinion is to explain a judgment or way of thinking about something. While stating opinion is one part of argumentation, an intelligent argument will not stop there. Argument will go much further. It will give an opinion (or claim) and then, vitally, support it with evidence.

Misconception #3: To Argue is to Have an Emotional Disagreement

Emotions often run high when we argue. Getting passionate about an issue is not a bad thing; in fact, if we didn't have passion for an issue, then why bother arguing about it? The problem with an intense emotion like anger is that it can often cloud our thinking. Instead of considering argumentation as something highly emotional, students should think of argument as a curious endeavor that they respectfully engage in with others who may not share their complete point of view.

Elements of Critical Thinking

This chapter is a culmination of the book in that it will use all of the analytical and critical thinking skills to allow you to create your own successful argument.

To sum up much of the book and prepare to make our own arguments, let's review the following Elements of Critical Thinking.

1. **Observations**

     From a series of observations, we can come to establish . . .

2. **Facts**

     From a series of facts, or from an absence of fact, we make . . .

3. **Inferences**

     Testing the validity of our inferences, we can make . . .

4. **Assumptions**

   From our assumptions, we form our . . .

5. **Opinions**

   Taking our opinions, we use evidence and the principals of logic to develop . . .

6. **Arguments**

   And when we want to test our arguments and to challenge the arguments of others, we employ . . .

7. **Critical Analysis**

   (Through which we challenge the observations, facts, inferences, assumptions, and opinions in the arguments that we are analyzing)

This book has hopefully allowed you to fully develop all of these elements of critical thinking. This chapter in particular will cover how to create your own arguments and then test their validity with critical analysis, particularly Aristotle's logic.

How to Create a Successful, Logical Argument

There are 6 simple steps that students can take to create their own arguments in undergraduate English courses. The very basic formula for a successful argument is as follows:

1. *Make a central claim in the thesis statement*

2. *Give reasons*

3. *Support the reasons with evidence*

4. *Connect the evidence back to your central claim*

5. *Acknowledge the opposition*

6. *Respectfully refute the opposition*

If you follow those steps, your argument is already on its way to being successful. Making sure it's a *good* reason with evidence that actually *supports* it is the part where students often make missteps.

Developing Your Central Claim and Thesis Statement

Your argument's central claim is essentially your *educated*, highly *focused* opinion on the topic, and you can develop an educated opinion on the topic through doing research. Your central claim on the topic will ultimately be expressed as your thesis statement.

Developing your central claim and ultimate thesis will have a movement like this:

Perform the Research Process → An Educated Opinion Emerges → Articulate the Central Claim → Create the Thesis Statement

NOTE: Once you have performed the research process and fully annotated and analyzed your sources, only then can you develop an intelligent opinion on the topic (refer to Chapters 3, 4, and 5 to learn about research, analysis, and synthesis, respectively).

The difference between an opinion and a thesis statement which includes your central claim is *focus*. On page 10, you will find Kevin A. Sabet's *Washington Times* article, "Colorado will show why legalizing marijuana is a mistake." His opinion, as revealed in this article, is that marijuana poses too many health and crime risks to become legal. His thesis that includes his central claim, on the other hand, is much more focused. The thesis statement of his argument is, "Colorado's experience [legalizing recreational marijuana], ironically, might eventually teach us that legalization's worst enemy is itself." Notice how much more *focused* the thesis is compared to his mere opinion.

When writing your own thesis, take care to make sure that it is not merely an overly generalized opinion, but a highly focused, specific, and debatable claim.

Writing a Debatable Thesis

The thesis statement should be a claim in which something is up for debate, not an undisputed fact. You should be able to defend your thesis in your future essay. Take the following statements as examples. What language is up for debate in the "debatable claim" statements?

Fact: It is unfortunate that each year in the United States, there are between 3 and 4 million homeless animals who will eventually become euthanized by shelters.

Debatable Claim: Pet owners who are not certified breeders should be required to spay or neuter their pets in order to cut down on the amount of animals euthanized in shelters every year.

Fact: Some students believe that professors have unfair rules about personal computer use in the classroom.

Debatable Claim: Professors not allowing personal computer use during lectures prevents students from learning and taking notes efficiently.

NOTE: See page 33 for specific information on how to write a successful thesis.

Question for Discussion

What is the authors' opinion in "3 Reasons Marijuana Legalization in Colorado is Good for People of Color" found on page 13? What is their thesis statement?

Giving Good Reasons

A reason is also called a *premise*. To put it simply, a reason is a claim that supports another, broader claim. When students settle on a thesis, they have probably already come up with many reasons for it. Reasons are what lead students to their claims in the first place. If you were to put *because* after your central claim, what comes after are all of your reasons. Other words that can link your claim to your reasons are *therefore, thus, consequently,* and *since*.

Once you develop your reasons, use the questions below to ensure that they will work successfully in your argument:

- **Are my reasons articulated accurately?** (Much like your thesis, your reasons should be as specific and clear as possible.)

- **Are my reasons relevant in light of my claim?** (Reasons should be *good* and *supportive*. If it's not a good enough reason to support the claim, revision is needed.)

- **Are my reasons logical in light of my claim?** (Reasons should logically support the claim. Reasons should not employ any errors in logic. For instance, if one overgeneralizes the issue or contradicts with another reason, revision is needed. See the section titled "Errors in Logic: How to Spot Them" in Chapter 4 for more information on errors in logic.)

- **Do I have enough reasons?** (Depending on the length of the argument, you want to actually limit your main reasons to around three. Any more than that will muddle your point and can be confusing to the reader.)

Question for Discussion

The central claim in the article *Lowering the Drinking Age is Not the Answer* on page 47 is obvious from the title, but what are the author's reasons? Use the questions above to decide if the reasons given are successful.

Providing Relevant Evidence

The verifiable information found during the research process is your evidence. Evidence is often called the *backing* or *grounds* for an argument. Each reason given should be well-supported with multiple bits of evidence; therefore, you want to place the evidence after each reason in your argument. Arranging it in this way will make your argument clearer for the audience.

Evidence comes in many forms: facts, interviews, case studies, expert testimony, anecdotes, statistical data, primary source material, etc.

When arranging evidence within your argument, use the questions below to ensure that the evidence is actually supportive.

- **Do I have enough evidence?** (The amount of evidence needed will depend on the reason. If the reason is overly strong, then you are burdened with providing more evidence. For instance, the claim, "All whales held in captivity should be released back into the wild" requires a lot of evidence.

On the other hand, the claim, "SeaWorld should consider releasing whales back into the wild if they are able to survive on their own" requires less evidence.)

- **Is my evidence current and accurate?** (This is where your credibility as an author or *ethos* comes into play. Your evidence should be trustworthy so that your audience will trust you in providing it.)

- **Is my evidence supportive?** (All evidence should directly and clearly support each reason. If the evidence employs an error in logic, like correlation equals causation, for instance, then you will have little ethos left, and your argument will be unsuccessful. See the section entitled "Errors in Logic: How to Spot Them" in Chapter 4 for more information on errors in logic.)

Question for Discussion

The article "3 Reasons Marijuana Legalization in Colorado is Good for People of Color" on page 13, gives three clear reasons for its claim. What evidence is presented to support those reasons? Use the questions above to decide if the evidence is successful in ultimately proving the central claim.

Activity

This activity will allow you to better visualize your argument's potential weaknesses. Most of your argument will contain two kinds of statements: claims and evidence. While your central claim is listed in your thesis followed by your reasons and respective evidence, every sentence in the body paragraphs will contain smaller claims and evidence to support them.

Write the letter *E* next to sentences that serve as evidence and the letter *C* next to sentences that serve as claims. Once you finish, count up each one and decide if you have too many unsupported claims or too much unclear evidence. Revise your draft accordingly.

Summarizing and Refuting the Opposition

Earlier in this chapter, in the section called "Misconceptions about Argument," Misconception #3 refers to the belief that arguments should be emotional. This misconception probably stems from the assumption that your audience vehemently disagrees with you, and it's your job to angrily respond. On the contrary, a reasonable, intelligent argument will:

a. give an unbiased, unemotional summary of the opposition's beliefs . . .

b. then respectfully refute it.

Summarize Opposing Views

You learned how to accurately summarize in Chapter 3, but *fairly* summarizing a view that you disagree with can be a challenge. When summarizing the opposition, take great care with your words, making sure that you are not using any slanted or charged language or appearing to be overly biased on the topic. You also want to avoid oversimplifying the issue and committing other errors in logic (see the section entitled "Errors in Logic: How to Spot Them" in Chapter 4 for more information on errors in logic).

Take a look at the following paragraphs that illustrate what a "biased" and "unbiased" summary of the opposition might look like.

Biased Summary

Supporters of eating an all-organic diet attempt to claim that these foods are healthier than their non-organic counterparts. They ignorantly believe that pesticides can cause cancer in humans, among other diseases, which ignores more current research that pesticides are safe to consume in small amounts. This misinformation is particularly dangerous for lower-income individuals who cannot afford to eat an all-organic diet; these scare tactics victimize the poor and are dangerous to the farming industry.

Unbiased Summary

Supporters of eating an all-organic diet argue that foods grown without the use of pesticides are healthier than their non-organic counterparts. They assert that pesticides can cause cancer in humans, among other diseases, and they see fault in the current studies that claim otherwise. Although organic foods tend to be more expensive, these groups say that the extra cost is worth it for good health.

Activity

Circle any charged or slanted language that you notice in the "biased" summary and then circle the words that make the paragraph fairer to the opposition in the "unbiased" summary.

Refuting the Opposition

A respectful rebuttal will typically involve refuting the opposition's *evidence*. The list below outlines the various ways that you can do just that.

- **Object to the "facts"** (Oftentimes data is up for debate, even if the opposition presents it as a fact. Object to the "facts" of the opposition's case, especially if you have your own data to refute them.)

  Example: "Most overweight people don't exercise enough." This is presented as a fact, but how would you reasonably object to it?

- **Question the ethos of the evidence** (When the opposition cites evidence from a less than credible source, it's important to call that into question. Personal anecdotes, studies with limited results, and testimony from non-experts on the topic are all bits of evidence that you may want to question.)

  Example: "Harry Tithes, sociology professor at New York University, claims that food vouchers for the poor will not offer enough nutritional variety." How could you question the credibility of this source?

- **Give counterclaims and examples** (When the opposition gives a bit of evidence to support some claim, you have the right to give evidence that directly refutes it. The evidence you give should ideally be better in some way—more current, more relevant, more thorough, etc.)

  Example: "Most college freshmen don't have enough personal responsibility to successfully manage their class schedules with a part-time job." How could you give a counterexample to refute this claim?

- **Question Statistics** (Since statistics are complex by nature, they are easy to misrepresent. Calling the opposition's statistics into question is a good strategy to undermine their argument.)

  Example: "A recent study showed that people who wear fitness trackers that count their daily steps weigh an average of 17 pounds less than people who don't, which shows that fitness trackers can help people lose weight." How could you question this statistic?

- **Criticize the breadth of evidence** (If you notice that the opposition only gives a few examples to support their claims, or perhaps selectively chooses examples that only prove their claim, then you can criticize that strategy to weaken their argument.)

  Example: "Several toddlers in Florida came down with the flu immediately after receiving the flu vaccine, so we should be cautious when considering this dangerous vaccine." How could you criticize the breadth of this evidence?

- **Criticize the relevance of the evidence** (If the opposition's evidence is not current, that is certainly a valid point of criticism. Calling for more up-to-date evidence from the opposition is a fair strategy for you to employ.)

  Example: "A 1976 poll of women showed that working moms do approximately 87% of the housework, while their husbands only do approximately 13% of the housework; this shows that marriages are simply not equal in terms of labor." How could you criticize the relevance of this evidence?

- **Explore the context of quotations** (A common rhetorical tool is to quote an expert out of content in order to convince an audience of your own interests. Exploring the context of quotations can help you to determine if the opposition is telling the whole truth.)

  Example: "The candidate told the reporter, "My marriage has seen better days," which had his supporters wondering if he can't be committed to his marriage, then can he be truly committed to helping our state?" How could you explore the context of the candidate's quotation to potentially refute the claim?

Using the Rhetorical Appeals in Your Argument

In Chapter 4: You are a Better Analytical Thinker Than You Realize, you learned about the three main rhetorical appeals, ethos, logos, and pathos, and how to use them to analyze an argument.

To briefly review, consider this quote from Aristotle in his book, *The Art of Rhetoric:*

> Of the modes of persuasion furnished by the spoken word there are three kinds. The first kind depends on the personal character of the speaker [ethos]; the second on putting the audience into a certain frame of mind [pathos]; the third on the proof, or apparent proof, provided by the words of the speech itself [logos].

In this section, you will learn how to use the rhetorical appeals to create your own persuasive argument.

Using Ethos to Persuade

When creating your own argument, your credibility and personal character is vital to being persuasive. If the audience doesn't trust you, then they won't buy into your argument. Since the audience may not know you personally (or even if they do!), you must write your argument in a way that evokes trust and credibility. Your tone, word choice, and conventions will all help you to develop ethos. Aristotle argued this point when he claimed, "Persuasion is achieved by the speaker's personal character when the speech is spoken to make us think him credible" in *The Art of Rhetoric.* Credibility is established within the speech, not by the speaker's character. While Aristotle is referring to an oral argument, the same can be applied to a written argument.

Aristotle tells us that there are three requirements to appearing credible:

1.   **Be Competent**

2.   **Be Empathetic**

3.   **Have Good Intentions**

How to Show Your Competence

You can show your competence as an author by **doing your research.** When you do your research, you become fully informed and knowledgeable on the topic. Of course, that needs to be evident in your argument. When you can fully develop examples and ideas, combine information from multiple sources, and write confidently on the issue, you will develop credibility, authority, and build ethos.

Using a sophisticated style is another way to appear competent and develop your ethos. This step cannot be overlooked. Quite simply, if your argument is not written in a sophisticated, professional style, you will not appear credible to the audience. Take great care with your word choice, conventions, and other stylistic details, and you can develop a strong ethos.

How to Be Empathetic

Merriam-Webster's Dictionary defines *empathy* as "the feeling that you understand and share another person's experiences and emotions." If you **respect the audience**, it will be much easier to empathize with them. Although at first glance, thinking of your audience and their feelings might appear to utilize a pathos appeal, your explicit respect and empathy for the audience will get them to trust you; it will develop your ethos. Respect the audience's viewpoints and it will make you seem more credible. Everyone thinks they have the answer, that they are right about an issue, so if you give into that tendency a bit, it will only help you to be persuasive and communicate your truth.

How to Illustrate Your Good Intentions

Good intentions are portrayed best if you **appear unbiased.** Of course you are *biased* on the issue; that's why you are arguing to begin with. However, you want to appear as unbiased as possible. This means that you should thoughtfully and respectfully consider alternative viewpoints, acknowledging *both* their strengths and weaknesses. Practicing empathy for the opposition will help you to achieve this.

Activity

Imagine for a moment that your major's curriculum is about to get cut from your university due to steep budget cuts. Write a brief paragraph persuading your classmates that your curriculum is worth keeping. Use ethos as your main persuasive strategy.

Using Logos to Persuade

Logos involves an appeal to logical reason. This rhetorical appeal encompasses the claims and evidence in any given argument. In *The Art of Rhetoric*, Aristotle referred to the logos appeal when he wrote, "Persuasion is effected through the speech itself when we have proved a truth or an apparent truth by means of the persuasive arguments suitable to the case in question." The structure and content of an argument influences its ability to be logical.

Earlier in this chapter, you learned how to utilize logos in the section entitled, "How to Create a Successful, Logical Argument." Those steps included creating a debatable thesis, giving good reasons and supporting them with evidence, among other things.

Here we will focus on the two **kinds of evidence** you should include to utilize the rhetorical appeal, logos:

1.   **Scholarly Sources**
2.   **Statistical Data**

Using Scholarly Sources to Persuade

In Chapter 3: You are a Better *Researcher* than You Realize, you learned how to locate, read, and actually use scholarly sources. You can use these sources to utilize logos. Because these sources are written by the experts and scholars in the field, the evidence will be powerful. These sources can often appeal to your audience's sense of logical reasoning. Logos is such a vital rhetorical appeal—developing a sense of logic will *also* give you ethos.

Articles, books, and other scholarly sources found through library research can appeal to your audience's sense of logical reason. Facts, examples, quotations, etc., are examples of the kinds of evidence that will persuade your audience. As an added bonus, these scholarly sources also give your argument some ethos. Note the tendency of the example below to appeal to *both* logos and ethos.

Argument with Scholarly Research:

The student tracking system commonly used in the United States public school system needs serious revision. For one thing, the higher tracks for higher performing students have a distinct advantage over the lower performing students in the lower tracks. In her article entitled, "Removing Instructional Barriers: One Track at a Time," Dr. Kimberly LaPrade, Professor of Education and Dean of the College of Education at Grand Canyon University, claims that "lower tracks may contain less of an intended curriculum . . . higher tracks had more variety and the teachers in those classes had more education and experience." Higher track students are receiving a higher level of teaching, and lower track students are receiving a lower level of teaching. These differences in teaching levels will obviously contribute to the self-fulfilling prophecy that allows the high performers perform even higher and the low performers perform even lower.

Source: LaPrade, Kimberly. "Removing Instructional Barriers: One Track at a Time." *Education* 131.4 (2011): 740–752.

Question for Discussion

- How does the argument above use scholarly research in a logical way?

Using Statistical Data to Persuade

Including statistical data in your argument is one of the best ways to appeal to your audience's sense of logical reasoning. Statistics can offer trustworthy, concrete proof that your audience will be persuaded by. What is perhaps most useful about statistical data is that it can be displayed in various ways to persuade your audience in the clearest way possible. The example below (also on student tracking in the public school system) utilizes statistical data in this way.

Argument with Statistical Data:

Not only has tracking proved to be contributing to the hamster wheel of poor education, giving higher performing students an edge over lower performing students, but the educators themselves have expressed concern. In their article entitled, "Perceptions and Attitudes Towards School Tracking: Structural Considerations of Personal Beliefs," Sociologists Frank Biafora and George Ansalone share the results of their surveys of school principals. The authors discovered that only 43.5% of principals thought that their teachers actually supported the tracking system, which means that over half of teachers probably do not support tracking, or at least their principals don't believe they do. The authors also found out that a whopping two thirds of principals did not want a tracking system at their school at all. If the education experts, principals and teachers, do not support the tracking system, shouldn't we seek to revise it?

Source: Biafora, Frank, and George Ansalone. "Perceptions and Attitudes of School Principals Towards School Tracking: Structural Considerations Of Personal Beliefs." *Education* 128.4 (2008): 588–602.

Question for Discussion

- How does the statistical data in the above example appeal to logos in particular?

Using Pathos to Persuade

The final way for you to create a persuasive argument is to utilize the pathos appeal. Evoking a particular emotion or set of emotions in the audience is a valid way to persuade an audience. An argument that uses excessive pathos, or pathos alone, could be problematic. But when done right, it can be very effective. Aristotle unpacked the effectiveness of utilizing pathos in *The Art of Rhetoric* when he said:

The emotions are all those feelings that change men as to affect their judgements, and that are also attended by pain or pleasure. Such are anger, pity, fear, and the like, with their opposites. We must arrange what we have to say about each of them under three heads. Take for instance the emotion of anger: here we must discover 1) what the state of mind of angry people is, 2) who the people are with whom they usually get angry, and 3) on what grounds they get angry with them.

The goal of pathos is to weaken the audience's ability to be critical and evoke powerful emotions among them, and there are two ways to successfully do that:

1.   **Know Your Audience**

2.   **Manage Your Presentation Style**

How to Show that You Know Your Audience

You will want to think carefully about your audience and what their belief and value systems might be. If you are in an undergraduate writing class, then your audience is your classmates. Understanding what they desire will help you to understand what kinds of evidence to use. It is recommended to **use concrete examples** that your audience will relate to when attempting to evoke an emotional response in them and utilize pathos. Writing about an issue or controversy with abstract examples only will not help to further your argument or utilize pathos effectively.

Question for Discussion:

1.   What does it mean for an example to be *concrete* and what does it mean for an example to be *abstract*?

The two arguments below illustrate the strength and emotion that comes from including a concrete example in your argument.

Argument with an Abstract Example:

A queer-inclusive literature curriculum in high school will help to further the LGBTQ rights movement. By including young adult novels that normalize alternative or queer sexual identities and behaviors like homosexuality, bisexuality, transgenderism, polyamory, asexuality, etc., in the high school curriculum, we can teach adolescents about equality in very subtle ways. Queer characters whose sexuality is *not* at the forefront of their character can particularly help to normalize these groups, giving students a sense that these characters are no different from the typical heteronormative ones they may read about more often.

Argument with a Concrete Example:

A queer-inclusive literature curriculum in high school will help to further the LGBTQ rights movement. By including young adult novels that normalize alternative or queer sexual identities like homosexuality, bisexuality, transgenderism, polyamory, asexuality, etc., in the high school curriculum, we can teach adolescents about equality in very subtle ways. Francesca Lia Block's popular 2004 young adult novel, *Weetzie Bat,* includes queer characters that embody this ideology. The main character, Weetize, is granted three wishes, one of which is for her male friend Dirk to find a male romantic partner. This moment in the novel is not dramatic; there is no emotional "coming out" story. Dirk's sexual preferences are revealed in the same way that heterosexual character's preferences are: without a label. Dirk is never even referred to as homosexual. Dirk's sexuality is simply not controversial, nor is it a major plot point in the novel. Queer characters whose sexuality is *not* at the forefront of their character can particularly help to normalize these groups, giving students a sense that these characters are no different from the typical heteronormative ones they may read about more often.

Question for Discussion:

- How does the argument that includes the concrete example help bring the issue to life compared to the one with only an abstract example?

How to Manage Your Presentation Style

Presenting your ideas in very particular ways can help to evoke emotion in the reader. The way you choose to present your evidence is meaningful. One way to manage your presentation style in order to evoke pathos is to **include concrete language**. Similar to using concrete examples, concrete language allows your reader to really *picture* the scenario; it allows them to *feel* the emotion that you are attempting to evoke.

The two arguments below illustrate the emotion that comes from including concrete language in your argument.

Argument with Abstract Language:

More state funding is needed for the public bus system. Without additional funding, the bus system will be forced to reduce the number of routes, giving people less opportunity to use the buses for transportation to and from their jobs, shopping for their families, etc. More funding is also needed for the bus to run later at night. People who work night shifts also need transportation. This recent reduction in funding seems to disproportionately impact lower-income people in particular.

Argument with concrete language:

More state funding for the public bus system is vital to the well-being of the citizens in this city. Without additional funding, the bus system will be forced to reduce the number of routes. This huge change will give the hardworking people of this city less opportunity to successfully contribute to their society. They will have less options for transportation to and from their jobs, less opportunity to grocery shop for their families, and other less opportunity to complete the vital activities of their day-to-day lives. Moreover, people who work night shifts should not be overlooked. One of the first routes to be cut was the late-night route, and this was a major affront to low-income people in particular, who are forced to work these less desirable jobs. This cut in funding seems like a classist decision that disproportionately affects lower-income people in particular.

Question for Discussion

1. Circle the concrete language you spot in the second argument. How does it compare with the language in the first argument?

Another way to manage your presentation style to evoke pathos is to **include a vivid anecdote**. This technique will humanize your argument, allowing your evidence to have an emotional impact.

Argument with No Anecdote:

There are currently only fourteen states in the United States that prohibit the use of hand-held cell phones while driving. While those fourteen states are showing progress, the rest of the country is lagging far behind. All of the United States should pass a law that would ban hand-held phone use while operating a vehicle. According to the 2015 Huffington Post article, "10 Statistics that Capture the Dangers of Texting and Driving," you are four times more likely to crash if you use a cell phone while driving.

Argument with an Anecdote:

All states in the United States should pass a law that would ban hand-held cell phone use while operating a vehicle. According to the 2015 Huffington Post article, "10 Statistics that Capture the Dangers of Texting and Driving," you are four times more likely to crash if you use a cell phone while driving. Knoxville mother Sharon Glasper knows this statistic all too well. The mother of seven-year-old Seraya, Glasper is in mourning since finding out that her young daughter was killed while riding the school bus. The bus driver was sending and receiving text messages at the time of the crash. He apparently swerved into another lane and crashed into another bus, sending his bus, filled with young school children, toppling over. Three were killed that day, and the driver was later found dead in his home. Horrific instances like this could be avoided through enforcing a hand-held cell phone ban while driving.

Questions for Discussion

1. How does the argument with the anecdote evoke pathos?
2. What rhetorical appeal is used in the first argument? Which is more effective in your opinion?

Testing the Logic of Your Argument

Now that we know how to create successful and logical arguments, it's time to test the logic of those arguments. You will also want to refer back to Chapter 4: You Are a Better *Analytical Thinker than You Realize* for argumentation tips like how to avoid (and spot) errors in logic.

Toulmin Method

The Toulmin Method is based off the work of philosopher Stephen Toulmin. In the 1950s, Toulmin did not appreciate the common way of looking at arguments, which at the time was to examine an argument's logic in a formal way. Instead, he takes an "audience-based" approach which students may find useful. When he first came up with this new way of thinking about argument, Toulmin used the courtroom as inspiration. In legal arguments, the lawyer is forced to assume that the audience does not agree and must tailor her argument accordingly. Using this courtroom model forces students, much like a lawyer arguing a case, to keep their audience in mind. This is useful because it allows us to constantly question our own assumptions about the topic, as well as consistently consider potential objections to our claims.

To remind you, here are the definitions for the key terms used in the Toulmin diagram below:

Central Claim: This is the statement that you are defending. It must be debatable, not a fact.

Qualifier: Examples of qualifying words are *sometimes* and *usually.* These words prevent the claim from being absolute and instead qualify it. A qualifier will be a phrase that includes words like these.

Exception: An exception is a condition in which you would not defend your central claim. Think of it like a special circumstance.

Reason: Reasons support or justify your central claim. Whatever comes after "because" in your claim is considered a reason.

Evidence: Evidence supports your reasons. It can be data, an anecdote, expert testimony, a case study, etc.

Refutation: This is where you seek to disprove the opposition. The refutation contains the objections and your respective rebuttal.

Objection: The opposition's claims. The objection is part of the refutation.

Rebuttal: Your response to the opposition's claims in an effort to refute them. The rebuttal is part of the refutation.

Toulmin Diagram Student Example and Activity

(Diagram format and layout adapted from *The Aims of Argument*, 7/e by Timothy W. Crusius and Carolyn E. Channell. Copyright © 2011 McGraw-Hill Companies, Inc. Reprinted by permission.

Decide whether or not you think the argument presented below is logically sound. Use the following questions as a guide:

- Does the claim *need* qualifiers or exceptions to be acceptable?
- Are the reasons relevant and supporting the claim?
- Are the reasons *actually* any good? Meaning, are they logical?
- Does the evidence *adequately* support the reasons?
- Are the objections refuted accurately? Or are they refuting something else?

The Central Claim: The president should raise the federal minimum wage.

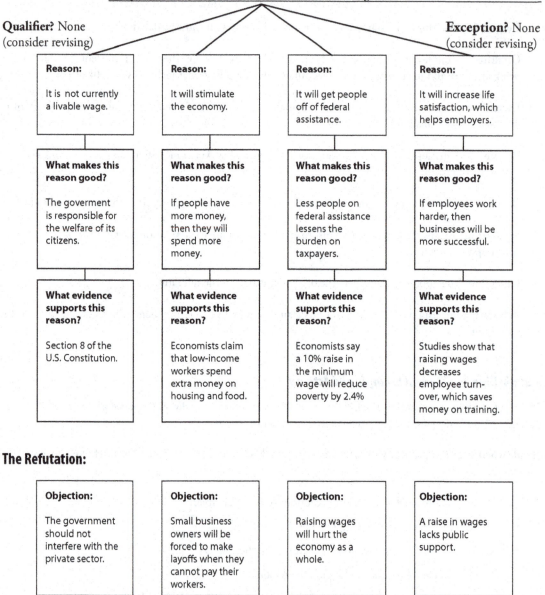

Qualifier? None
(consider revising)

Exception? None
(consider revising)

Reason: It is not currently a livable wage.	**Reason:** It will stimulate the economy.	**Reason:** It will get people off of federal assistance.	**Reason:** It will increase life satisfaction, which helps employers.
What makes this reason good? The goverment is responsible for the welfare of its citizens.	**What makes this reason good?** If people have more money, then they will spend more money.	**What makes this reason good?** Less people on federal assistance lessens the burden on taxpayers.	**What makes this reason good?** If employees work harder, then businesses will be more successful.
What evidence supports this reason? Section 8 of the U.S. Constitution.	**What evidence supports this reason?** Economists claim that low-income workers spend extra money on housing and food.	**What evidence supports this reason?** Economists say a 10% raise in the minimum wage will reduce poverty by 2.4%	**What evidence supports this reason?** Studies show that raising wages decreases employee turn-over, which saves money on training.

The Refutation:

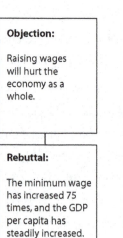

Objection: The government should not interfere with the private sector.	**Objection:** Small business owners will be forced to make layoffs when they cannot pay their workers.	**Objection:** Raising wages will hurt the economy as a whole.	**Objection:** A raise in wages lacks public support.
Rebuttal: Federal assistance programs already interfere.	**Rebuttal:** 3 out of 5 small business owners support a gradual increase in wages.	**Rebuttal:** The minimum wage has increased 75 times, and the GDP per capita has steadily increased.	**Rebuttal:** A 2013 poll suggests that the majority of Americans support an increase in minimum wage.

Partner Activity

Use the Toulmin Diagram below to test the effectiveness of your own argument. Fill in the blanks with the parts of your written argument. Ask a partner to test your argument's logic using the questions from the previous example.

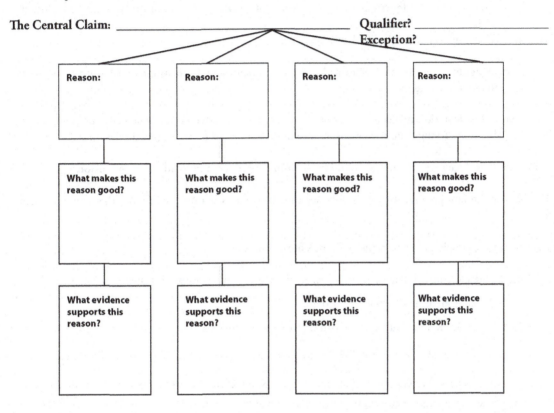

The Central Claim: _____   Qualifier? _____

Exception? _____

Reason:

Reason:

Reason:

Reason:

What makes this reason good?

What makes this reason good?

What makes this reason good?

What makes this reason good?

What evidence supports this reason?

What evidence supports this reason?

What evidence supports this reason?

What evidence supports this reason?

The Refutation:

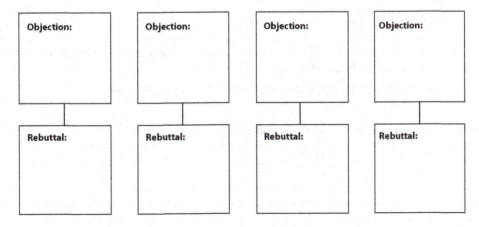

Objection:

Objection:

Objection:

Objection:

Rebuttal:

Rebuttal:

Rebuttal:

Rebuttal:

Aristotle's Theory of the Syllogism

Another way to make sure that your argument (and others' arguments) is logically sound is to develop a syllogism for it. Merriam-Webster fully defines this term as follows:

A deductive scheme of a formal argument consisting of a major and a minor premise and a conclusion.

Merriam-Webster offers a more simple definition also:

a formal argument in logic that is formed by two statements and a conclusion which must be true if the two statements are true.

While Aristotle's definition might be a bit more sophisticated (he refers to the statements as "premises," for instance), all of the varying definitions work well to understand if your own argument is logical.

A syllogism has three parts: the **major premise**, the **minor premise**, and finally, the **conclusion**.

The major and minor premises are two general statements that are presumed to be true. They contain a shared term.

Here are some examples, the first being Aristotle's most common:

1.   All men are mortal, and Socrates is a man; therefore, Socrates must be a mortal.

     a.   Major Premise: All men are mortal.

     b.   Minor Premise: Socrates is a man (shared term is "man").

     c.   Conclusion: Socrates is a mortal.

2.   No dogs have feathers, and all Labradors are dogs; therefore, no Labradors can have feathers.

     a.   Major Premise: No dogs have feathers.

     b.   Minor Premise: All Labradors are dogs.

     c.   Conclusion: No Labradors have feathers.

3.   If your child does not receive all of her vaccines, she is putting her health at risk. Your child received all of her vaccines; therefore, she will be healthy.

     a.   Major Premise: If your child does not receive all of her vaccines, she is putting her health at risk.

     b.   Minor Premise: Your child received all of her vaccines.

     c.   Conclusion: She will be healthy.

Activity

Create a syllogism for the following argumentative passages, then decide if the argument is logical or not. There may be several possibilities for a syllogism for each passage. See the argumentative passage below to use as a guide.

Argumentative Passage and Syllogism Example

With an attendance policy in place, some students will feel obligated to attend class in order to earn points, and then start to doze off, watch YouTube videos, text on their cell phones, etc. This behavior distracts other students who are actually trying to pay attention to the lecture and learn the material. This kind of behavior isn't uncommon in classrooms *without* an attendance policy, so can you imagine the severity of this issue if we allowed students to earn points *just for attending?* Perhaps a more comprehensive "participation grade" is needed instead of an attendance policy. After all, students who actively participate in class are proven to learn more effectively than students who are more passive.

Major Premise: Distracting students prevents them from learning effectively.

Minor Premise: Mandatory attendance policies will force some students to attend class and distract other

students.

Conclusion: Mandatory attendance policies prevent students from learning effectively.

Is the conclusion logical? Explain: No. While attendance policies might prevent *some* students from learning, that won't be true for all students. Not all classes will have students who seek to distract others, and not all students will actually be distracted. The argument needs more qualifiers for it to be logical.

Another option for this passage:

Major Premise: Attendance policies prevent students from learning effectively.

Minor Premise: Students will learn effectively with a participation grade.

Conclusion: Participation grades should be given instead of having an attendance policy.

Is the conclusion logical? Explain: Yes. Although the major premise needs a qualifier, the conclusion gives a logical and reasonable alternative to an attendance policy. Since student learning is a high priority in college, and it has been proven that participation helps students to learn better, this conclusion seems logical.

1. Attendance policies should really only be used in case of lab work since it can *only* be completed in class. Otherwise, students should be treated as responsible adults instead of helpless children. Responsible adults know that if they don't show up to work, then they could get fired. Similarly, students understand that not showing up to class puts them at risk for failure since they are missing important material. Some students are okay with taking a risk, and they may have to pay the consequences. Professors have to be willing to give failing grades; this is a normal part of academia. Administrators shouldn't seek to control students through a mandatory attendance policy, but instead encourage them to succeed by attending class willingly.

Major Premise: _____

Minor Premise: _____

Conclusion: _____

Is the conclusion logical? Explain:_____

_____

2.   Attendance policies can only help students, particularly first year students. It has been proven that students who attend class regularly perform better in those courses. First year students in particular are less likely to attend class. This could be due to a sudden lack of adult or parental supervision like they are accustomed to in high school. First year students often have difficulty balancing their newfound freedom with their academic responsibilities. Obviously, these students need attendance policies more than any other group.

Major Premise: _____

_____

Minor Premise: _____

_____

Conclusion: _____

_____

Is the conclusion logical? Explain:_____

_____

3.   Attendance policies are simply too much work for professors. Professors not only have to take roll and re-calculate grades based on attendance, but they also have to engage in quibbles with students about their attendance or lack thereof. Students may claim to have attended class when they didn't, and professors could potentially make a mistake while taking roll. Getting into tense conversations with students about their attendance takes time away from professors to do class prep work, grading, or research. This excessive amount of housekeeping work causes professors undue stress which ultimately only hurts students.

Major Premise: _____

_____

Minor Premise: _____

_____

Conclusion: _____

_____

Is the conclusion logical? Explain:_____

_____

Partner Activity

Create several syllogisms for your own argument: one for your thesis and one for each body paragraph. Trade with a partner and decide whether or not their logic is faulty or not.

Argument Peer Revision

STEP ONE—Examining the Introduction Paragraph

Does the paragraph make the controversy and argument clear? Meaning, does it explain WHAT is up for DEBATE and clearly show why your argument is worth considering?

Does it provide an adequate CONTEXT? Or perhaps some background information? Is that working well? Why?

STEP THREE—Examining the Thesis Statement:

Does the student offer a debatable thesis? Or is it merely stated as a fact?

Is the thesis focused and clear?

Does the thesis offer a direction for the essay?

STEP FOUR—Examining the Body Paragraphs:

Does the student provide enough evidence to support their claims and reasons?

Is the evidence appealing to a variety of rhetorical proofs?

Does the student draw significant conclusions based on their source material?

Are the sources *good* ones?

STEP FIVE—Considering Organization and Style:

Are the paraphrases and quotations integrated properly? Circle any dropped quotes

Is the organizational plan easy to follow?

Are there accurate transitions between paragraphs?

Are there any stylistic problems that need correcting?

STEP SIX—Examining the Conclusion:

Does the conclusion merely summarize the essays points? If so, give them some suggestions for improvement.

Does the conclusion look to the future in some way? Is that strategy working?

Does the conclusion synthesize their points and make their argument clear?

CHAPTER 7

You are a Better *Editor* than You Realize

As discussed in a previous chapter, revision is a vital part of the writing process. Consciously deciding to revise your work with a calm demeanor, not a panicky "I'm the worst writer in the world!" attitude will allow you to see that you CAN write successful essays.

As the writing process continues, students will begin to feel more confident in their essay's content. They start to feel like they are drawing some nice conclusions based on relevant and reliable research. Developing your ability to analyze issues and controversies is more than half the battle. The final bit of crafting a successful essay is organization and style, and that comes during the revision and editing process.

In this chapter, we will cover tips for editing and revision, organization, grammar reminders, integrating research clearly, and word choice. Although content and ideas should be any writer's first priority, if your communication isn't as clear, concise, and accurate as it could be, then your ideas can't really shine.

Starting the revision process far in advance of the essay's due date will help you to avoid that anxious feeling. Hopefully using the strategies detailed in this chapter will allow you to see that you are a better writer than you realize.

Writing Crisp, Succinct Sentences

Sometimes students get caught up in an assignment's required word count, and other times they may write how they speak. Either way, those issues can both cause excessive wordiness, which can water down your brilliant ideas. With too many words, your content becomes muddled and not as clear as it could be.

Take this example for instance:

> Having a part time job while you are in school is a really good idea for most people because they learn responsibility and they also learn how to balance their school work, studying for tests, and doing homework with another, equally as important responsibility so they ultimately become a better, more well-rounded person when they graduate.

Believe it or not, that is not a run-on sentence (more on how to spot those later). It is actually grammatically correct, but so wordy that the reader can't be certain what the exact point is. We can easily reduce the amount of words to make the sentence clearer. The sentence is 56 words total, so let's see how brief we can get it without sacrificing content:

> Most students should have a part-time job because it allows them to develop a sense of responsibility and work-life balance, which will make them more well-rounded upon graduation.

Even though the words were cut almost in half, the sentence has the same meaning, and even uses much of the same language to convey the point. This sentence is much easier for the reader. Don't make your audience work hard to understand your point!

Revision Practice: Wordiness

In the space below each excessively wordy sentence, rewrite it in a clearer, more succinct way while maintaining their integrity of meaning:

1. The attendance policy, for most traditional students, can be, and should be, eliminated because it is excessive and many students think that it is unfair to both themselves and non-traditional students as well.

   Word Count: 33

   _____

   _____

   _____

   _____

   (New Word Count:____)

2. Only allowing three unexcused absences without excuses should be re-thought-out by teachers because many times, a student cannot get an excuse from a doctor for things like a simple cold or something else similar to that situation.

   Word Count: 37

   _____

   _____

   _____

   _____

   (New Word Count:____)

3.   Lowering a student's grade by 5 percentage points on the final grade is a very major change in the actual grade that the student has earned on their other work that they put effort into so this seems like too significant of a punishment for only missing one extra class beyond the three absence rule, therefore the attendance policy should be considered for revision by administrators.

Word Count: 66

_____

_____

_____

_____

(New Word Count:_____)

Correcting Common Errors

We learn grammar skills throughout elementary, middle, and perhaps even high school, but frankly, all of the rules are really difficult to remember! By the time we get to college, we are more focused on the quality of our content than simple grammatical mistakes. Even though most of the mistakes that we go over in this chapter won't interfere with the reader's understanding, they can certainly be distracting. Here are some common errors and how to fix them:

1.   **Using the pronoun *you* unnecessarily**

Unless the student is writing a letter or wants to address the reader directly, they should avoiding using the pronoun, "you." When we talk with our friends, we use the term casually, and they understand based on our demeanor and tone that we mean the *universal* "you," but when we communicate in written form, tone and demeanor cannot be identified by the reader, and we should choose a more accurate pronoun. Substituting *he or she* for you is a good idea, or students can use *one* as an alternative. Even when the writer is referring to him or herself, they should go ahead and use *I.* Here are some sample sentences that illustrate an incorrect use of the word "you."

Justifying the cost for produce grown with no pesticides or other chemicals can be complicated. Eating organic vegetables is a priority for many people, but you may want to reconsider if you have a low income.

Changing "you" to "shoppers" and adding the pronoun "they" is actually more clear, and the writer's intent is more obvious to the reader.

Justifying the cost for produce grown with no pesticides other chemicals can be complicated. Eating organic vegetables is a priority for many people, but shoppers may want to reconsider that they have a low income.

Removing the "you" made the sentence seem much less aggressive. ,The writer isn't preaching for the reader to change, but instead explaining exceptions, and the second version of that sentence makes that clear.

2.   **Using comma splices, which is a major grammatical sin!**

A comma splice is a serious error, but often students don't remember the comma rules that they learned years prior, so teachers can understand how they can happen. The *pause rule* might be a reason why college students often have comma splices in their writing. Comma splices can occur when a student isn't thoughtful about comma placement, and instead, puts a comma where one might *pause* in conversation. This "pause rule" is a fallacy and should generally be avoided.

A comma splice occurs when a comma is placed between two complete sentences or independent clauses. A period or semi-colon is the appropriate punctuation in those cases.

In order to avoid comma splices, it's important to understand the components of a sentence. A complete sentence has a subject, a verb, and expresses a complete thought. The same goes for an independent clause, which can stand alone with no supplemental words or punctuation.

The sentence below is complete, and here is how we know:

> I want cereal for breakfast.
>
> Identify the verb first (want)
>
> Who or what is performing the verb? That's the subject (I)
>
> Then decide if it expresses a complete thought. (It does—cereal for breakfast.)

Take a look at the sentence below, which uses a comma incorrectly.

> **Comma Splice**: The authors in this article claim that their study has groundbreaking results, those results were later published in *The New York Times* newspaper.

If you break apart the sentence, you will see that on both sides of the comma, we have an independent clause, or what could be thought of as a complete sentence. There are various ways to correct the error, but two options are listed below:

> **Correct Version**: The authors in this article claim that their study has groundbreaking results. Those results were later published in *The New York Times* newspaper.

> **Correct Version**: The authors in this article claim that their study has groundbreaking results; those results were later published in *The New York Times* newspaper.

To clarify, only use a semi-colon if the two independent clauses are closely related.

Correcting one of the most common errors in college English is actually a lot simpler than students realize. You just have to know what makes up a complete sentence.

3.   **Using excessive pronouns**

This error is called *unclear pronoun reference.* Here are some examples of pronouns: *it, those, her, him, she, he, they, you, them.* Pronouns are a way to add variety to a sentence and take the place of nouns. Using too many pronouns in a sentence or paragraph can be misleading or unclear for the reader. See the example below:

> This article examines an odd event that occurred in the jungles of Belize in the summer of 2002. It is significant because it reminds readers to recycle and always think about the environment.

The pronoun in this sentence is "it." Can you tell which noun "it" is referring to? There are a couple of options, which makes the sentence unclear. If the author instead wrote:

> This article examines an odd event that occurred in the jungles of Belize in the summer of 2002. The event is significant because it reminds readers to recycle and always think about the environment.

4.   **Using possessives and plural possessives incorrectly**

Once students understand and review the rules of possessives, they see how easy it really is. Only place an apostrophe *before* the "s" when you want to make a *singular* noun possessive. Place an apostrophe *after* the "s" for a *plural* noun that you wish to make possessive. See some example sentences below.

> Five different authors contributed to an article on global warming.

> The five authors' article details why global warming is such a significant controversy.

The possessive rules get tricky when we think about words that end in "s" that we also want to make possessive. When this happens, we DO NOT add an extra apostrophe "s," but instead just put an apostrophe after the "s" that is already there. Take a look at the two sentences below:

> WRONG: Welcome to Alexis's Birthday Party!

> RIGHT: Welcome to Alexis' Birthday Party!

Another commonly misused possessive is "its" and "it's." "Its" is the possessive form of "it," and "It's" is the contraction for "it is." See the example sentences below:

> The dog chased its tail.

> It's the hottest day of the year.

5.   **Using *affect* and *effect* correctly**

This rule is simple, but it is easy to mix up. *Affect* is a verb. *Effect* is a noun. It's that simple! See the example sentences below:

The effects of the hurricane are still felt in the rural town.

The hurricane certainly negatively affected the rural town.

These five errors are the most common easily-corrected errors in student writing. Once you finish a draft or two of your essay, consider checking for these errors in particular. Microsoft Word has the capability to search for terms in the document, so try doing a search for, say, "affect" to make sure you are using it correctly. Or, try searching for various pronouns to make sure that the sentence is clear. Revision and editing can be a tedious process, but a polished, successful essay will be the result.

Colloquialism: Avoid Using Informal Language

For most academic assignments, students should avoid using colloquialism, slang, or other forms of informal language. Similarly, idioms or figures of speech should also be left out. Instead, students should strive to use the most accurate word possible, and since colloquial language is open to interpretation, it's best to stick with a slightly formal tone and word choice.

The sentence below uses colloquial language:

Cops have a bad rep because of all the things going down lately, but who knows if it's justified or not!

Although the sentence makes logical sense and could be understood by almost anyone whose first language is English, it lacks the formality needed for an academic environment. Remember the rhetorical triangle? Students should consider the audience and context of the assignment. If this was a sentence in an e-mail to a friend, then the language is just fine, but if the sentence is in an academic essay, then it's not formal enough to be taken seriously.

Below is a revised, more formal version with no colloquial language:

Police officers have a bad reputation because of all the violence they seem to perpetuate, but I'm not sure if it's justified or not.

Word Choice: The Most Accurate Word Is the Best Word

The English language is bountiful with choices. Words like "amazing" and "awesome" are used so frequently in today's culture that they no longer have much meaning. To be awe-struck, which is what *awesome* actually means, can simply not be used to describe a TV show or ice cream. A description of a near death experience, now that could be described as *awesome*. When you are writing anything, but particularly academic or professional assignments, strive to use the most accurate word possible.

If a student writes "This was a great article for my project" in an annotated bibliography, what do you think she actually means? There are so many options. The word is too vague to convey any meaning. She could have used *useful, informative, current, detailed, thorough, accurate,* etc. All of those words have a very particular meaning and are much more specific than merely the adjective "great."

Revise the sentences below to be more formal, with no colloquialism, slang, or vague language.

1.   The author barely brushes the surface of this controversial topic.

   _____

2.   The author paints a bleak picture of our society in the next decade.

   _____

3.   The new bill lit a fire within the protestors.

   _____

4.   The cons of this issue are immense.

   _____

5.   On the other side of the fence, many think alcohol should be more regulated.

   _____

   _____

6.   The news anchor does not journey into much detail on the current immigration controversy.

   _____

   _____

7.   The article goes into the next issue too quickly, and I couldn't get what he was saying.

   _____

   _____

8.   The senator made it clear that she is for gay marriage during her speech.

   _____

   _____

Question for Discussion

- What editing strategies work best for you? What have you tried in the past that hasn't worked?